Children's Bulletins

 Abingdon Press

CHILDREN'S BULLETINS

ISBN 0-687-06507-0

04 — 10 9 8

MANUFACTURED IN THE UNITED STATES OF AMERICA

Contents

COLOR THIS PICTURE

WORD SEARCH

```
N H A G U E S T H S
O D R G S T V J U N
I B V D X G S E E H
T C H L R U A V A C
A J W Y S H I G O O
V B D E C G G L H D
L G J C R M L C E N
A C A O O E I T E T
S Z F C C R A W R F
O Z G T E E D O V I
G I O J H V H A K K
J R C C Y S O X C R
```

WORD LIST

CHEATED	COLLECTOR
FORGIVEN	GUEST
JERICHO	JESUS
SALVATION	SHORT
ZACCHAEUS	

ANSWERS

WORD SEARCH

```
J G O S H N S
K K A H R
I V O Y W J B T
F R W A B R U S G
E D O A E C A L U
T I L E G R J Y E
E O O C J G X H S
D A M R B I G A T
G Z Z F C O V
C R A W R O V
G Y S O X C R
```
(SALVATION, GUEST circled)

WORD MATCH

TAX ——— CLIMBED
TREE ——— PEOPLE
CHEATED ——— COLLECTOR

UP A TREE

BASED ON LUKE 19:1-10

TODAY SALVATION HAS COME TO THIS HOUSE.

Scripture for Today

Luke 19:9b

LESSON—Zacchaeus was not a well-liked man because he was the chief tax collector. He took money from the people who needed it badly. When Zacchaeus heard that Jesus was coming to Jericho he wanted to see him. Because he was small, Zacchaeus climbed a tree so he could see Jesus. When Jesus saw Zacchaeus in the crowd he called to him and told him that he wanted to go home with him. Jesus forgave Zacchaeus for treating the people wrong. Zacchaeus changed the way he lived and began treating others better.

MATCH THE WORDS

tax	climbed
tree	people
cheated	collector

CONNECT THE DOTS

Where did Zacchaeus go so he could see Jesus?

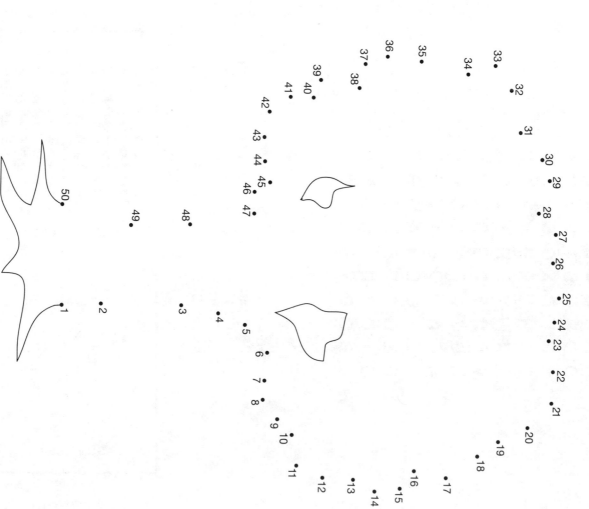

COLOR THIS PICTURE

WORD SEARCH

```
H S N Y P B O S L C I V
X A L F L V O C W C Z P
P P B E S W M J A F B J
H E S I P C A W E A G N
W S A K H C H O A J S M
R Y L C J S A F L T X I
U H M E E E R Z W K E S
P W L S R W B J B K I R
K Q E V B R A R P Q S S
W G W L K A A V M C K Y
C S M E L D I U G B G B
C R D T P S K E Q J V B
K Q A R Z Q X W I Z E O
K R O A M L G Z Z A L R
X E L O X O P O W X A H
```

WORD LIST

ABRAHAM
BLESS
PEACE
SHIBAH
WELLS

ALTAR
ISAAC
QUARREL
WATER

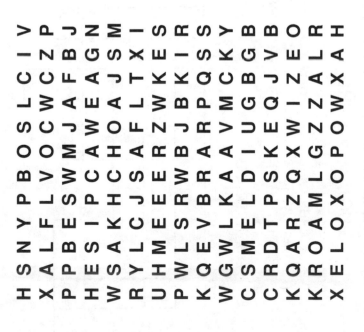

CROSSWORD PUZZLE

```
        D
        U
   W    W    I S A A C
A R G U E    L
   T    E    T
   E   L O T A
   R
D I S C O V E R
```

WORD SEARCH

```
H                       X
R                       E
B                       L
Y                       O
S                       X
S                       O
R                       P
E                       O
E                       W
M                       X
H                       A
U                       H
...
```

ANSWERS

From *Children's Bulletins*. Copyright © 1992 Abingdon Press. Used by permission.

2

ISAAC MAKES PEACE

BASED ON GENESIS 26:17-33

Scripture for Today

I AM THE GOD OF YOUR FATHER ABRAHAM. DO NOT BE AFRAID, FOR I AM WITH YOU.

Genesis 26:24b

LESSON—Isaac moved into an area where water was scarce. He had his servants dig new wells. The men of Gerar wanted to argue with Isaac about use of the water. Isaac would not argue about the wells and their use and moved to Beersheba. Again, his servants dug wells and another dispute arose over whose water it was. Isaac prayed to the Lord for help. The men who had been arguing with him came and made peace with him because they realized he was a man of God.

CROSSWORD PUZZLE

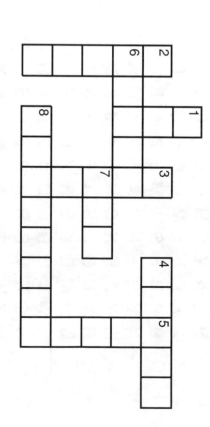

ACROSS CLUES

4. HE SOUGHT THE LORD
6. FUSS AND FIGHT
7. IMPORTANT O.T. MAN
8. FIND

DOWN CLUES

1. SHOVELED OUT
2. CLEAR DRINK
3. WHERE WATER COMES FROM
5. A PLACE TO PRAY

MAZE

Help Isaac find a place to dig for water.

START

DIG HERE!

DRAW A PICTURE

COLOR THIS PICTURE

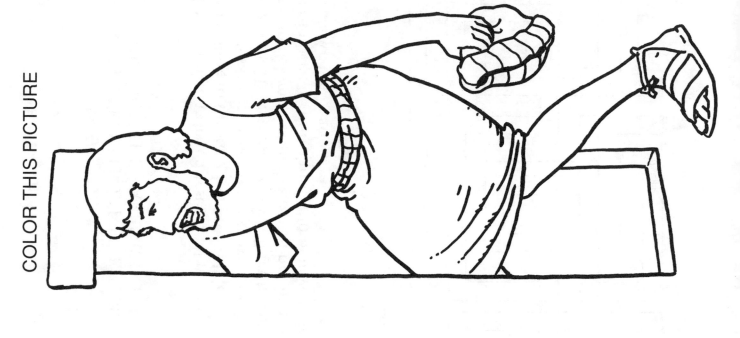

DRAW A PICTURE OF WHAT YOU THINK
HEAVEN WILL BE LIKE

CROSSWORD PUZZLE

ANSWERS

LET ME IN!

Scripture for Today

MAKE EVERY EFFORT TO ENTER THROUGH THE NARROW DOOR.

Luke 13:24

LESSON—Someone asked Jesus what was necessary to do to belong to the kingdom of God. Jesus told them to enter the narrow door, where few go in, and to follow him. He said that many will try to take a shortcut to heaven, but that they will not be allowed to enter in because only those who believe in Jesus will be allowed in heaven.

MAZE

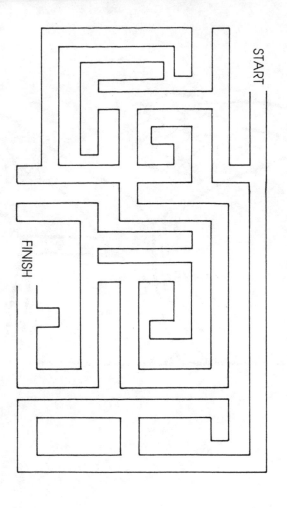

START

FINISH

CROSSWORD PUZZLE

ACROSS CLUES

6. USED TO CHEW FOOD
7. NOT INSIDE
8. A BIG MEAL
10. PEOPLE WHO DO WRONG
11. NOT FIRST
12. FINISHED A DRINK
14. SKINNY

DOWN CLUES

1. WHERE WE LIVE
2. GO INTO
3. NUMBER ONE
4. BEATING ON THE DOOR
5. ROADS
9. A LOT OF CRYING
12. CLOSE THIS BEHIND YOU
13. _____ OF GOD

COLOR THIS PICTURE

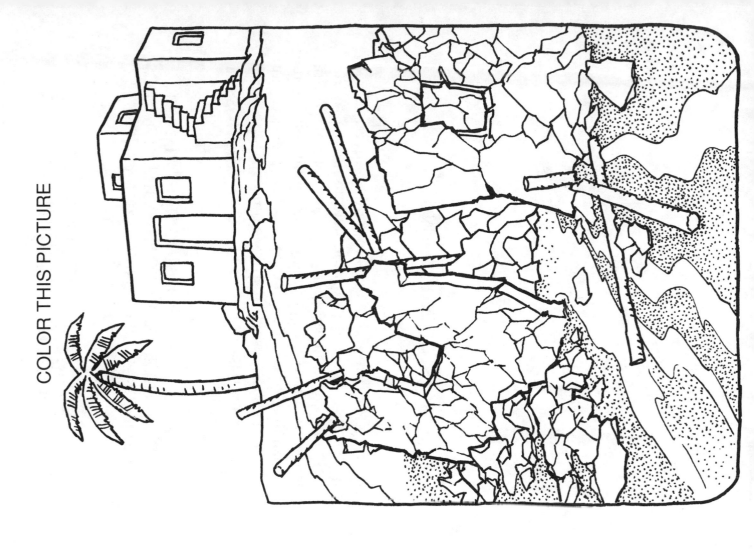

WORD SEARCH

```
K I K F Q V B R P H
Q S E C S W G W K S
V L M C R K Y K C I
L S M E D A C I G L
B S G B C O S R D O
P R D S R B K H E O
J V A N B K U Q R F
Z N Q I X W I I Z
D E O K N W O A L M
L G Z Z A L R X E D
L O X O P O W X A H
X Q P H B B Z R V H
```

<u>WORD LIST</u>

BUILD   RAIN
CRASH   ROCK
FELL   SAND
FOOLISH WINDS

WORD SEARCH

```
K I K F Q V B R P H
Q S E C S W G W K S
V L M C R K Y K C I
L S M E D A C I G L
B S G B C O S R D O
P R D S R B K H E O
J V A N B K U Q R F
Z N Q I X W I I Z
D E O K N W O A L M
L G Z Z A L R X E D
L O X O P O W X A H
X Q P H B B Z R V H
```

ANSWERS

From *Children's Bulletins.* Copyright © 1992 Abingdon Press. Used by permission.

4

BUILDING A HOUSE

BASED ON MATTHEW 7:24-27

Scripture for Today

EVERYONE WHO HEARS THESE WORDS OF MINE AND PUTS THEM INTO PRACTICE IS LIKE A WISE MAN WHO BUILT HIS HOUSE ON THE ROCK.

Matthew 7:24

LESSON—Jesus told his disciples that it was wise to build their life on his words because they were true and strong. He told his disciples a story about two men who built houses. One built his house on sand and when the rain came the house fell with a great crash. The other man built his house on a rock so that when the wind and rain came the house stood strong in the storm.

CONNECT THE DOTS

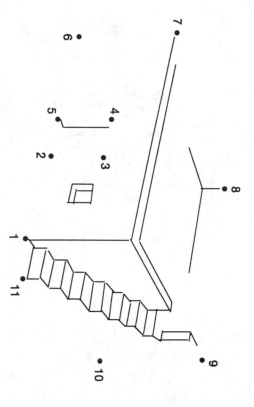

DRAW A PICTURE OF TODAY'S STORY

COLOR THIS
PICTURE

WORD SEARCH

V X L F V O W C Z P P S W J Y
F B J H P V C E G N E W P K S
C T O J N M I R Y S J I F L O
X U E D H I M L I E T Z W K R
S O P N E L N A L Y S W J B P
K T N I K L R E M A Q V B R E
P Q H E S P A S W A G G W K L
H T I A F V M E C K S E Y C S
M E D I N G B G H B C T R D P
K E J V B K K Q R Z Q X E W I
Z E O K O A S M L G Z Z A R L
R X E L O X O P O W X A H X Q

WORD LIST

FAITH   HEALED
LEPROSY   MASTER
NINE   ONE
PITY   PRAISE
TEN   THANKS
VILLAGE

WORD SEARCH

V X L F V O W C Z P P S W J Y
F B J H P V C E G N E W P K S
C T O J N M I R Y S J I F L O
X U E D H I M L I E T Z W K R
S O P N E L N A L Y S W J B P
K T N I K L R E M A Q V B R E
P Q H E S P A S W A G G W K L
H T I A F V M E C K S E Y C S
M E D I N G B G H B C T R D P
K E J V B K K Q R Z Q X E W I
Z E O K O A S M L G Z Z A R L
R X E L O X O P O W X A H X Q

WORD SCRAMBLE	FILL IN THE BLANKS
JESUS	1. JESUS
LEPROSY	2. CALLED
WELL	3. PRIESTS
THANKS	4. MAN

ANSWERS

5

TEN HEALED OF LEPROSY

BASED ON LUKE 17:11-19

Scripture for Today

RISE AND GO; YOUR FAITH
HAS MADE YOU WELL.

Luke 17:19

LESSON—Jesus was traveling throughout the land to tell people about God. As he came into one village, ten men who had leprosy came out to meet him. They called out and asked Jesus to have pity on them and to help them. Jesus granted their wish and told them to go and show themselves to the priests. They all went away, but one came back and thanked Jesus for healing him. Jesus asked why only one had returned to say thank you for making him well. Jesus told the one man who had returned that his faith had made him well.

FILL IN THE BLANKS

1. _____ cared about the ten sick men.

 David   Paul   Jesus

2. They _____ out to Jesus and asked him

 called   ran   crawled

 to heal them.

3. Jesus told them to go and show themselves to the

 _____ .

 priests   mayors   doctors

4. Only one _____ came back to thank Jesus.

 man   woman   priest

DRAW A PICTURE

UNSCRAMBLE THE WORDS

SUSEJ

ROSEYPL

LEWL

SHANTK

COLOR THIS PICTURE

WORD SEARCH

```
W J B K I K Q V B R P Q S S
W G W K V M C K Y C S M E D
I L G B S G B C R D D P K E
J V E B B A K Q R Z Q A X W
I Z E V A O M K O A M L E S
G Z Z A I N L A R X E L R D
O X O P O T D J R W X E A H
Y X Q P H B B E A Z I B R V H
F C V C T B R R Z B D I N N
Z K H N A E D O L K E W M X
O O Q L N A S T A S U Q C Q
I T W D P T W O T D B E K Q
```

WORD LIST

BANDAGED	JERICHO	ROAD
BEAT	LEVITE	ROBBERS
DEAD	PRIEST	SAMARITAN

CROSSWORD PUZZLE

WORD SEARCH

```
W J B K I K Q V B R P Q S S
W G W K V M C K Y C S M E D
I L G B S G B C R D D P K E
J V E B B A K Q R Z Q A X W
I Z E V A O M K O A M L E S
G Z Z A I N L A R X E L R D
O X O P O T D J R W X E A H
Y X Q P H B B E A Z I B R V H
F C V C T B R R Z B D I N N
Z K H N A E D O L K E W M X
O O Q L N A S T A S U Q C Q
I T W D P T W O T D B E K Q
```

ANSWERS

From *Children's Bulletins*. Copyright © 1992 Abingdon Press. Used by permission.

HELPING ONE ANOTHER

BASED ON LUKE 10:25-37

Scripture for Today

LOVE THE LORD YOUR GOD
WITH ALL YOUR HEART AND WITH ALL YOUR
SOUL AND WITH ALL YOUR STRENGTH
AND WITH ALL YOUR MIND; AND
LOVE YOUR NEIGHBOR AS YOURSELF.

Luke 10:27

LESSON—A man was traveling down the road to Jericho when robbers trapped him and took all of his clothes and possessions. They beat him so much that he was half dead. As he lay there a priest walked by, but instead of stopping to help the injured man he crossed over to the other side of the road. Another man came by and saw the man, and did the same thing the priest had done. Both of them ignored the man's need for help.

A third man, who lived in Samaria, came by and saw the man lying in the road. He felt sorry for him and stopped to help him. He treated the man's wounds and bandaged him up. Then he put the man on his own donkey and took him to the next town to get him help. He left him with an innkeeper and gave him money to take care of the man until he was well again. Even though he did not live near the man who had been hurt, the Samaritan became that man's neighbor.

CROSSWORD PUZZLE

<u>ACROSS CLUES</u>

3. AN ANIMAL TO RIDE
4. USED TO COOK WITH
7. A HOLY MAN
8. A LOT OF NICKELS AND DIMES
9. PEOPLE WHO STEAL

<u>DOWN CLUES</u>

1. CUTS
2. SOMEONE WHO LIVES NEARBY
5. A MEMBER OF THE TRIBE OF LEVI
6. ONE WHO TENDS A HOTEL
7. GO BY
9. WHAT WE TRAVEL DOWN ON A TRIP

COLOR THIS PICTURE

WORD SEARCH

```
Y I S K L T F M F T R S Y G N
M D M N P R E E I G O V D A H
N B E S E A A N Y P O S L C A
I V X T V L V F V O W C Z J
P A S K W A J F B J H P I
C E G R N N W R B N K C O J L
M R Y J F L A X U R E H M E E
Z W K S P L S R W J E W B K I
K Q V B R D P Q D S S A E W G
W K V M C K E Y C S M E D D D
I G B G B C R E D P K E J V B
K Q R Z Q X W I F Z E O K O A
```

WORD LIST

BREAD
DRANK
FEED
RAIN
RAVINE

DEW
ELIJAH
MEAT
RAVENS

ANSWERS

WORD SEARCH

```
Y I S K L T F M F T R S Y G N
M D M N P R E E I G O V D A H
N B E S E A A N Y P O S L C A
I V X T V L V F V O W C Z J
P A S K W A J F B J H P I
C E G R N N W R B N K C O J L
M R Y J F L A X U R E H M E E
Z W K S P L S R W J E W B K I
K Q V B R D P Q D S S A E W G
W K V M C K E Y C S M E D D D
I G B G B C R E D P K E J V B
K Q R Z Q X W I F Z E O K O A
```

TRUE OR
FALSE

1. TRUE
2. TRUE
3. FALSE
4. TRUE

FED BY THE BIRDS

BASED ON 1 KINGS 17:1-6

Scripture for Today

YOU WILL DRINK FROM THE BROOK,
AND I HAVE ORDERED THE RAVENS
TO FEED YOU THERE.

1 Kings 17:4

LESSON—God often talked to Elijah and told him what to do and always cared for him. God had said there would be no rain for several years in the place Elijah had been living. God told Elijah to travel east and hide in the ravine near Jordan. He told Elijah that he would drink water from the brook and that ravens would bring him the food he needed to eat. Elijah believed God and followed his instructions. God did as he had promised and provided for the prophet.

TRUE OR FALSE

1. God said it would not rain for years.

2. God sent Elijah, the prophet, into hiding.

3. Elijah drank water from the brook in a gold cup.

4. The ravens brought food as God had promised.

CONNECT THE DOTS

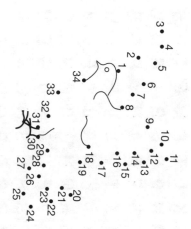

DRAW A PICTURE OF SOMETHING GOD HAS DONE FOR YOU

COLOR THIS PICTURE

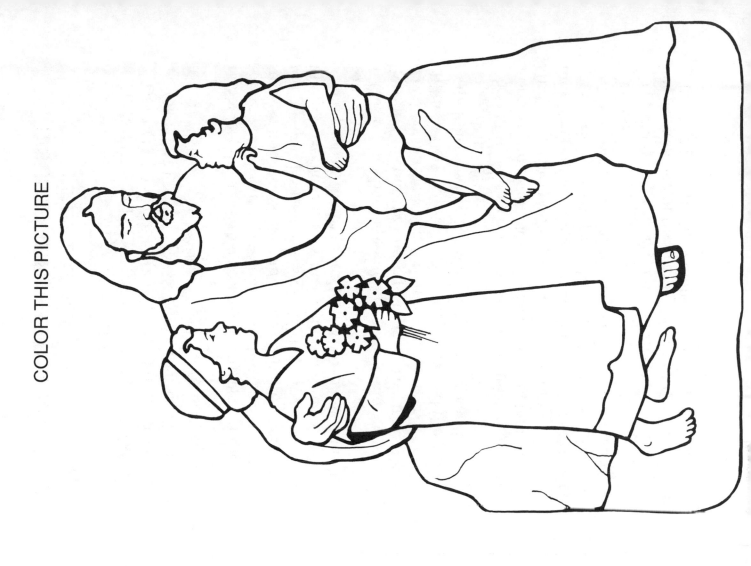

WORD SEARCH

```
O A M L G Z Z A L R X E
L L O X C C O P O W X A
H I K H X H O Q P H B B
S H T I E Z I M R V H Y
U X A T N A M L E O W H
S A F N L G V E D K L Q
E L O R D E D E X R T G
J Q C F C S V O N T E Z
B N Z K N A D L M K W N
M X O Q Y A R P L N S T
```

WORD LIST

CHILDREN	COME
HANDS	HEAVEN
JESUS	KINGDOM
LITTLE	ME
PRAY	

JESUS AND THE CHILDREN

BASED ON MATTHEW 19:13-15

Scripture for Today

LET THE LITTLE CHILDREN COME TO ME,
DO NOT HINDER THEM, FOR THE KINGDOM
OF HEAVEN BELONGS TO SUCH AS THESE.

Matthew 19:14

LESSON—Imagine that you lived long ago in the land where Jesus lived. You would probably have heard stories about Jesus, the same stories that we hear today—how Jesus healed sick children and how he fed hungry people and how he loved everyone. You would probably want to see Jesus yourself, wouldn't you?

This is just what happened to some children who lived in the country where Jesus lived. One day their mothers heard that Jesus was near. The children were happy. The mothers carried the babies in their arms while the older children ran and skipped along.

Soon they saw a crowd of people around Jesus. They stopped and listened to his voice and watched his kind face. They wanted to get closer to him. But as they tried to push their way through the crowd, some friends of Jesus stopped them. "Jesus does not have time for you today," they said. "He is busy and he is very tired."

The children were sad. They started to turn away, but Jesus smiled at them and held out his arms. "I love children," he said. The children were very happy.

UNSCRAMBLE THE WORDS

JUSES

CNERDHIL

RAPY

TITLEL

DRAW A PICTURE

COLOR THIS PICTURE

WORD SEARCH

```
K I K Q G V B R P Q S S
W G W O K H V M C K Y C
V F D S M S E R V E E D
I E O G B T G A B C R D
P K G O A E J V L B K Q
R Z Q E D X W I Z T E O
K O A M T S L G Z R H T
Z A L R X A E L E O A Y
X O P O M W B T X B A H
X Q P H E B A L L B Z R
V H Y X N W O E E W H A
F K L Q L O R X T S G Q
```

WORD LIST

EAT	FOODS
GOD	HEALTHY
MEN	SERVE
TABLE	VEGETABLES
WATER	

WORD SEARCH

```
K I K Q G V B R P Q S S
W G W O K H V M C K Y C
V F D S M S E R V E E D
I E O G B T G A B C R D
P K G O A E J V L B K Q
R Z Q E D X W I Z T E O
K O A M T S L G Z R H T
Z A L R X A E L E O A Y
X O P O M W B T X B A H
X Q P H E B A L L B Z R
V H Y X N W O E E W H A
F K L Q L O R X T S G Q
```

ANSWERS

AN EATING CONTEST

BASED ON DANIEL 1:3-15

Scripture for Today

Daniel 1:12

PLEASE TEST YOUR SERVANTS FOR TEN DAYS.

LESSON

The king had made Daniel and his people prisoners. To make them more like his people, the king ordered the men to eat and drink heartily. Daniel wanted his men given a chance to show how healthy their diets were. After ten days of eating vegetables and the right food, Daniel's men were healthier than the king's men.

MAZE

Help Daniel's men find their way to good food.

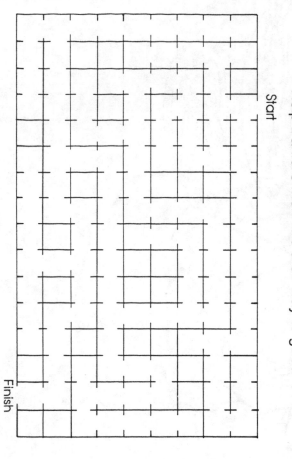

Start

Finish

DRAW A PICTURE OF TODAY'S LESSON

COLOR THIS PICTURE

DRAW A PICTURE OF TODAY'S STORY

CROSSWORD PUZZLE

WORD CHOICE

1. BEGINNING
2. DAY
3. DARK
4. CREATURES
5. IMAGE

ANSWERS

```
E A R T H
A     E
R     C R E A T E D
T     R       V
H     B L I G H T S
      E       E
      N       D
S A W
```

GOD CREATES THE WORLD

BASED ON GENESIS 1:1-27

Scripture for Today

IN THE BEGINNING GOD CREATED THE HEAVENS AND THE EARTH.

Genesis 1:1

LESSON—In the beginning God created everything. Everything that He made was good. God created the sun and moon. He created the land and the sea. He created all of life and it was good.

CHOOSE THE RIGHT WORDS

1. In the _____ God created the heavens and earth.

    start   beginning   afternoon

2. He called the light, _____ .

    day   morning   noon

3. He called the _____ , night.

    spooky   dark   evening

4. God created all of the _____ .

    creatures   stuff   pollution

5. God created man in his own _____ .

    time   image   house

CROSSWORD PUZZLE

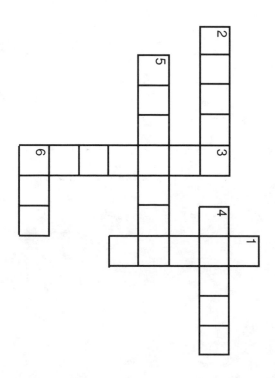

ACROSS CLUES

2. WHERE WE LIVE
4. NOT DARK BUT _____
5. MADE
6. GOD _____ THAT IT WAS GOOD

DOWN CLUES

1. THESE FLY
3. THE SKIES ABOVE

WORD SEARCH

```
W H A F K L Q L O R X T
G Q E C C P F C V T Z B
O N T L Z R R K N A D Y
L H K R C W U I M X O T
W Q C L U R H M E N S I
T A U I Q M I O B S C C
Q I L T R W P C R L T D
P W O L B E E K N E S
Q F S Z P L J S T X S D
D C I T U O H S Q S N O
```

WORD LIST

CIRCLE	CITY
CRUMBLED	HORNS
JERICHO	PRIESTS
SHOUT	TRUMPETS
WALL	

WORD SEARCH

```
W H A F K L Q L O R X T
G Q E C C P F C V T Z B
O N T L Z R R K N A D Y
L H K R C W U I M X O T
W Q C L U R H M E N S I
T A U I Q M I O B S C C
Q I L T R W P C R L T D
P W O L B E E K N E S
Q F S Z P L J S T X S D
D C I T U O H S Q S N O
```

WORD CHOICE

1. LORD
2. TRUMPETS
3. SIX
4. PEOPLE
5. LORD

ANSWERS

From *Children's Bulletins*. Copyright © 1992 Abingdon Press. Used by permission.

11

TAKING THE CITY FOR GOD

Scripture for Today
SHOUT! FOR THE LORD
HAS GIVEN YOU THE CITY!

Joshua 6:16b

LESSON—God promised Joshua that the city of Jericho would belong to him. Instead of fighting a battle with weapons of war, God told Joshua to take his men and march around the city. They did this for six days. On the seventh day, as the priests sounded their trumpets and the people shouted, the walls of the city crumbled and fell down. The city was Joshua's as God had promised.

CHOOSE THE RIGHT WORDS

1. The _____ told Joshua to go to Jericho.

   travel agent   King   Lord

2. The priests blew their _____ as instructed.

   trumpets   noses   cover

3. The men marched around the wall for _____ days.

   three   six   seven

4. The _____ shouted and the walls fell down.

   children   elephants   people

5. The _____ had done what he promised and the city was captured.

   King   Lord   Mayor

DRAW A PICTURE OF TODAY'S LESSON

COLOR THIS PICTURE

DRAW A PICTURE

From *Children's Bulletins*. Copyright © 1992 Abingdon Press. Used by permission.

THE BOY JESUS LEARNS ABOUT GOD

BASED ON LUKE 2:40-52

Scripture for Today

DIDN'T YOU KNOW I HAD TO BE IN MY FATHER'S HOUSE?

Luke 2:49b

LESSON—Mary and Joseph had journeyed to Jerusalem to celebrate the Feast of Passover. On their way home no one knew where young Jesus was. They looked for Jesus three days and found him sitting among the teachers in the temple. He had gone there to learn more about God.

MAZE

Help Jesus' family find him.

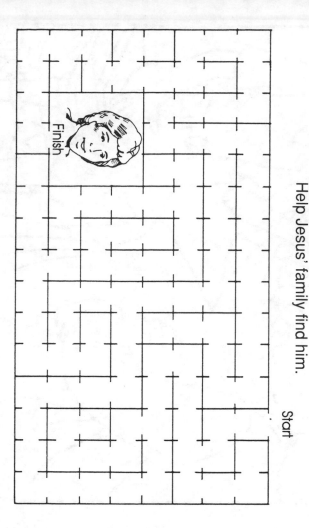

Finish

Start

CHOOSE THE RIGHT WORDS

1. Jesus and his family had gone to _____ for Passover.

       Jericho   Bethany   Jerusalem

2. They had come to celebrate _____.

       Passover   Easter   Mother's Day

3. On the return _____ they missed Jesus.

       trip   ride   ticket

4. They looked for _____ days for Jesus.

       five   ten   three

5. They found Jesus at _____.

       the cafe   the hospital   the temple

TRUE OR FALSE

1. Mary did not go to Jerusalem.

2. They had come to attend a feast.

3. Jesus wanted to learn more about God.

4. It took three days to find Jesus.

5. Jesus was sleeping when they found him.

COLOR THIS PICTURE

WORD SEARCH

```
W O B E K R Q F L S
E Z P L S A X D I C
L G P I Q L N O G E
T E Y E K L L K H R
H C A P O I L F T I
G D L R T P T O O F
I G E O S S L Q R X
N O J L U I W E U D
T D X F Z D S S U K
D T F O P U S Y L E
```

<u>WORD LIST</u>

CLOUDS   EGYPT
FIRE   GOD
ISRAEL   LED
LIGHT   LORD
NIGHT   PEOPLE
PILLAR

WORD SEARCH

```
W O B E K R Q F L S
E Z P L S A X D I C
L G P I Q L N O G E
T E Y E K L L K H R
H C A P O I L F T I
G D L R T P T O O F
I G E O S S L Q R X
N O J L U I W E U D
T D X F Z D S S U K
D T F O P U S Y L E
```

ANSWERS

From *Children's Bulletins*. Copyright © 1992 Abingdon Press. Used by permission.

GOD PROTECTS HIS PEOPLE

BASED ON EXODUS 13:17-22

Scripture for Today

SO GOD LED THE PEOPLE AROUND BY THE DESERT ROAD TOWARD THE RED SEA.

Exodus 13:18

LESSON—The Pharaoh had kept the Israelites captive for a long time. When he finally freed the people they were in great danger. God protected His people and led them into safety.

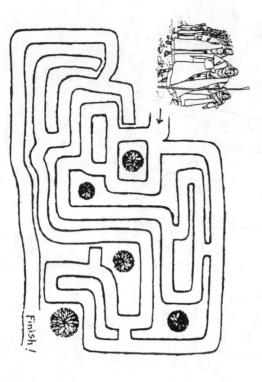

MAZE

Help the Israelites find their way to freedom.

Finish!

DRAW A PICTURE OF TODAY'S LESSON

COLOR THIS PICTURE

WORD SEARCH

```
M D R S W L W D S S
J M Y H R K R D L N
A E E L M E R T T A
X T R O A L X Q E
U S E U C H R L U L
I J A M S H Y K E C
C E Q N P A A C E S
B S U O G L L N O T
B U T Z P R E E T G
Q S G H C N Y L M S
```

WORD LIST

ANGRY   CLEANS
HOLY   JERUSALEM
JESUS   MARKET
MERCHANTS   SELLERS
TEMPLE

WORD SEARCH

```
M D R(S W L W D S)S
J M Y H R K R D L N
A E E L M E R T T A
X T R O A L X Q E
U S E U C H R L U L
I J A M S H Y K E C
C E Q N P A A C E S
B S U O G L L N O T
B U T Z P R E E T G
Q S G H C N Y L M S
```

WHO? WHAT?

1. JESUS

2. PEOPLE SELLING
   ANIMALS AND THINGS

3. HE RAN THEM OUT
   OF THE TEMPLE

ANSWERS

JESUS CLEARS THE TEMPLE

BASED ON JOHN 2:13-16

Scripture for Today

HOW DARE YOU TURN MY FATHER'S HOUSE INTO A MARKET!

John 2:16c

LESSON—Jesus went to the temple to worship. What he found made him angry. People were selling cattle, sheep, doves, and other things. Jesus told them they could not make his Father's house a marketplace and ran them off.

WHO? WHAT?

1. Who went to the temple to worship God?

_____

2. What did he find there?

_____

3. What did Jesus do?

_____

DRAW A PICTURE OF TODAY'S STORY

COLOR THIS
PICTURE

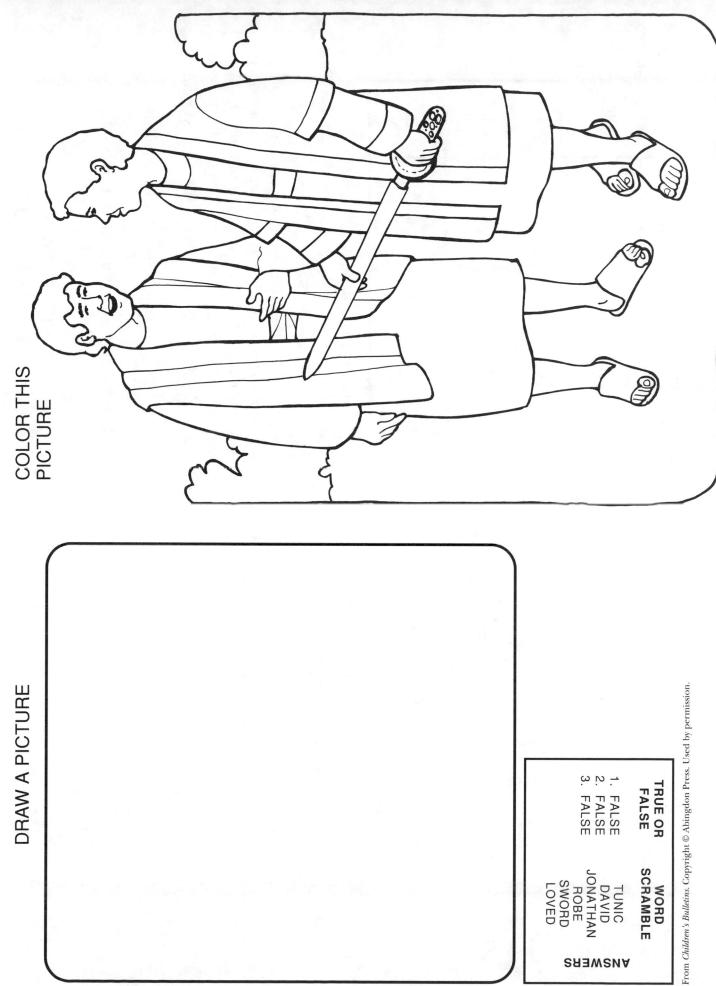

DRAW A PICTURE

TRUE OR
FALSE

1. FALSE
2. FALSE
3. FALSE

WORD
SCRAMBLE

TUNIC
DAVID
JONATHAN
ROBE
SWORD
LOVED

ANSWERS

TRUE FRIENDS

BASED ON 1 SAMUEL 18:1-4

Scripture for Today

JONATHAN BECAME ONE IN SPIRIT WITH DAVID.

1 Samuel 18:1b

LESSON—Jonathan became a very close friend of David's. They had the same kind of likes and dislikes. They promised to always be friends. Jonathan gave David his favorite robe and sword to show how much he cared for his friend.

MAZE

Help David find his friend Jonathan.

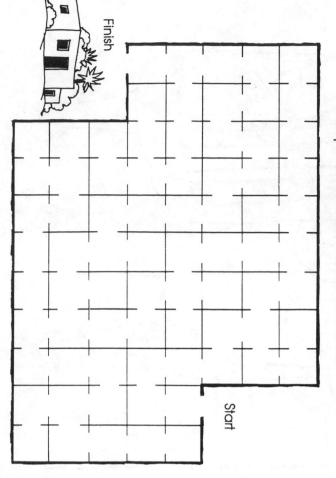

Finish

Start

WORD SCRAMBLE

NUTIC

DIVAD

NAOJHNAT

BORE

SODWR

VOLED

TRUE OR FALSE

1. David had been talking with Goliath before he saw Jonathan.

2. David and Jonathan were brothers.

3. David gave Jonathan his favorite bow.

CONNECT THE DOTS

COLOR THIS PICTURE

DRAW A PICTURE OF WHAT YOU THINK THE
MEN SAW WHEN JESUS HEALED THEM

CROSSWORD PUZZLE

WORD
SCRAMBLE

1. crowd
2. blind
3. Jesus
4. saw

ANSWERS

TWO BLIND MEN SEE

BASED ON MATTHEW 20:29-34

Scripture for Today

Matthew 20:32b

WHAT DO YOU WANT ME TO DO FOR YOU?

LESSON—Two blind men were sitting by the roadside. They heard that Jesus was coming their way. As Jesus approached them they called out to him. Jesus asked what they wanted. They asked for him to heal them and that they might see again. Jesus felt sorry for them and when he touched them they could see again.

UNSCRAMBLE THE LETTERS

1. A large ———————— followed Jesus.

 (ROWCD)

2. Two ———————— men were sitting by the roadside waiting

 (NIBLD)   for Jesus.

3. They called out to ———————— to restore their sight.

 (UESJS)

4. Jesus touched them and they ———————— again.

 (WSA)

CROSSWORD PUZZLE

ACROSS CLUES

3. NOT STANDING BUT ————
5. SON OF GOD

DOWN CLUES

1. A STREET
2. MADE WELL
3. THE MAN DESIRED TO HAVE THIS RETURNED TO HIM
4. WHAT YOU SEE WITH

DRAW A PICTURE

COLOR THIS PICTURE

DRAW A PICTURE OF TODAY'S LESSON

WHAT DO YOU THINK?

1. YES
2. YES
3. NO

ANSWERS

THE FISH AND THE COIN

BASED ON MATTHEW 17:24-27

Scripture for Today

TAKE THE FIRST FISH YOU CATCH;
OPEN ITS MOUTH AND YOU WILL FIND
A FOUR-DRACHMA COIN.

Matthew 17:27c

LESSON—A tax collector came to Jesus and the disciples and asked him to pay taxes. Jesus told Peter to go fishing and the first fish he would catch would have enough money in its mouth to pay the taxes. He did as he was told and Jesus was right.

WHAT DO YOU THINK?

1. The tax collector was after money?

2. People were watching to see what Jesus would do?

3. Peter went to the fish market and bought a fish?

CONNECT THE DOTS

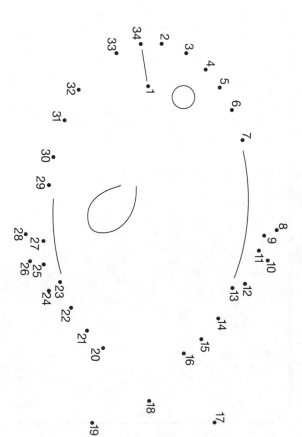

COLOR THIS PICTURE

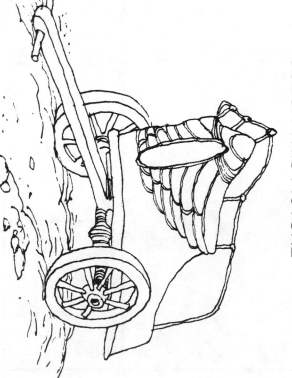

COLOR THIS PICTURE

WORD SEARCH

U H M E Z W K P S P Y L S W J
B K I K Q E H V B R P C Q S S
W G W K V A V M C K Y C R S M
E D I G R B E I G B C R D E P
K E J I V B K L L Q R Z Q X M
W I S Z E S O P P D K O A M L
G E Z E I Z R A L M O R X E L
E O X N L A O P O W E E X A H
X Q N P Y B H B D B Z T R R V
H E Y E X O M O W H A F K L Q
R L D O R X G U T G Q C F C V
T Z B N Z K N A H D L K W M X

WORD LIST

GOD   MERCY

EVILDOER   PRAYED
HUMBLE
PHARISEE   TEMPLE
SINNER

From Children's Bulletins. Copyright © 1992 Abingdon Press. Used by permission.

18

THE TAX COLLECTOR

BASED ON LUKE 18:9-14

Scripture for Today

EVERYONE WHO EXALTS HIMSELF WILL BE
HUMBLED, AND HE WHO HUMBLES HIMSELF
WILL BE EXALTED.

Luke 18:14c

LESSON—There is no room for pride in ourselves
where Jesus is concerned. He tells a story about a
Pharisee who stood in the temple and thanked God
that he was not a lowly, cowardly tax collector. He had
a lot of pride as he rambled on about what he was.
The tax collector got up and asked God to have mercy
on him for he was a sinner. Which person do you
think God was happier with?

CONNECT THE DOTS

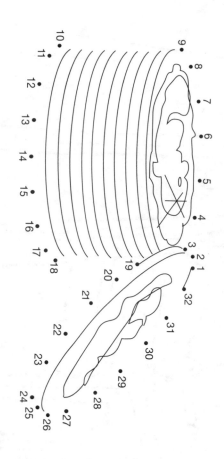

FIND THE WORD

temple   proud   mercy   humble

1. Two men went to the ———— to pray.

2. One man was very ———— of what he had done.

3. One man asked God to show ———— on
   him for he was a sinner.

4. The tax collector was very ———— in spirit.

DRAW A PICTURE OF TODAY'S STORY

COLOR THIS PICTURE

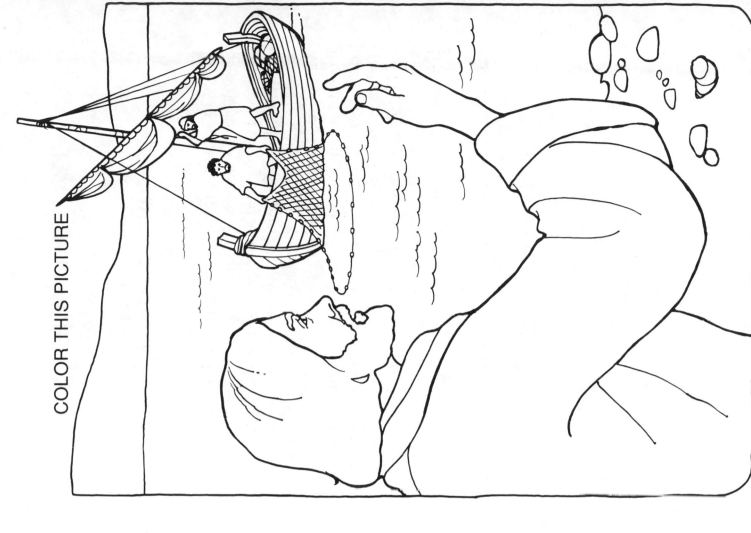

WORD SEARCH

```
S N Y P O S L C I W V X
L F V O W C Z P E N P S
B W J F B J H R E P C E
G O N W K C D T O J M F
R Y A J F N S L X U I H
M E Z T A W F K S S P L
S W J B K O I K H Q V B
R P Q S L P S E W G W K
V M C L E K R Y C S M E
D I O T G M B G B C R D
P W E K A E J V B K Q R
Z R Q N X W I Z E O K O
```

<u>WORD LIST</u>

ANDREW   BOAT
FISHERMAN   FOLLOW
NETS   PETER

From *Children's Bulletins.* Copyright © 1992 Abingdon Press. Used by permission.

TWO FOLLOW JESUS

BASED ON MATTHEW 4:18-22

Scripture for Today
COME, FOLLOW ME.

Matthew 4:19

LESSON—One day when Jesus was walking by the Sea of Galilee, he saw two brothers named Peter and Andrew. He watched as the men threw their fishing nets into the water and dragged in the fish in their nets. He walked up to the two men and said, "Come, follow me. I will make you fishers of men." Going on from there, he saw two more brothers, James and John, also fishing. Jesus invited them to go with him and they did. The men understood that Jesus was asking them to join him and be an important part of his earthly ministry. The men followed Jesus and became disciples of Christ.

UNSCRAMBLE THE WORDS

LGAILEE

REPET

IFSHMEREN

ROBTERHS

TOBA

CROSSWORD PUZZLE

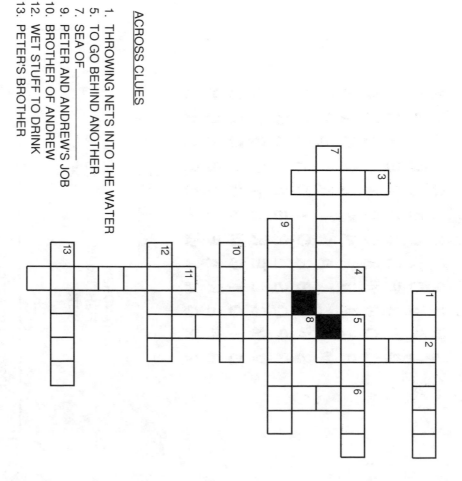

ACROSS CLUES

1. THROWING NETS INTO THE WATER
5. TO GO BEHIND ANOTHER
7. SEA OF _____
9. PETER AND ANDREW'S JOB
10. BROTHER OF ANDREW
12. WET STUFF TO DRINK
13. PETER'S BROTHER

DOWN CLUES

2. ANOTHER NAME FOR PETER
3. YOU RIDE IN IT ON THE WATER
4. USED TO CATCH FISH
6. A BODY OF WATER
8. FATHER OF JAMES AND JOHN
11. STROLLING ALONG

COLOR THIS PICTURE

WORD SEARCH

```
I Q N O K L K L M F T O S N Q
X J R I S E I W A U T X O F Z
S E S U R F M K R D T I F O P
G V U Y E E L A Y E T S P S I
R E B N W P H G R C G H X Y W
A I D P M E H T E T Y X O A L
V L Y X V H R A P H Y P D F
E E Q P F S R G U F P A H N S
W B S U T U I P M O X O D B R
C V D L S N O F R V F W M W I
N I C E U O D H T G I O Z C M
M H R X X N R U O M T N K H W
```

WORD LIST

BELIEVE	DAYS
FATHER	FOUR
GRAVE	LIFE
MARTHA	MARY
MOURN	RESURRECTION
RISE	TOMB

WORD SEARCH

```
I Q N O K L K L M F T O S N Q
X J R I S E I W A U T X O F Z
S E S U R F M K R D T I F O P
G V U Y E E L A Y E T S P S I
R E B N W P H G R C G H X Y W
A I D P M E H T E T Y X O A L
V L Y X V H R A P H Y P D F
E E Q P F S R G U F P A H N S
W B S U T U I P M O X O D B R
C V D L S N O F R V F W M W I
N I C E U O D H T G I O Z C M
M H R X X N R U O M T N K H W
```

FILL IN THE BLANKS

1. TWO
2. ILL
3. JESUS
4. WENT
5. LAZARUS

ANSWERS

LAZARUS RETURNS FROM DEATH

BASED ON JOHN 11:17-43

Scripture for Today

I AM THE RESURRECTION AND THE LIFE.

John 11:25a

LESSON—Lazarus was the brother of Mary and Martha. He became ill and died. His sisters and their friends were very sad. When word of Jesus' friend, Lazarus, reached him, Jesus went to the home of the sisters. By the time he got there, Lazarus had been buried.

Martha told Jesus that if he had been there when Lazarus was ill he would not have died. Jesus said to her, "I am the resurrection and the life. He who believes in me will live, even though he dies; and whoever lives and believes in me will never die. Do you believe this?"

Martha said that she did. Jesus went to the tomb and told the men to take away the stone that sealed the tomb. He prayed to his Father, God, and called to Lazarus to come out of the grave. With that, Lazarus came out of the tomb and was alive again. Jesus told them to take off the grave clothes and let him go home.

FILL IN THE BLANKS

Lazarus   ill   two   went   Jesus

1. Lazarus had _____ sisters.

2. He became _____ and died.

3. When _____ heard of Lazarus' death he was sad.

4. Jesus _____ to the home of Mary and Martha.

5. He told _____ to come out of the grave.

CONNECT THE DOTS

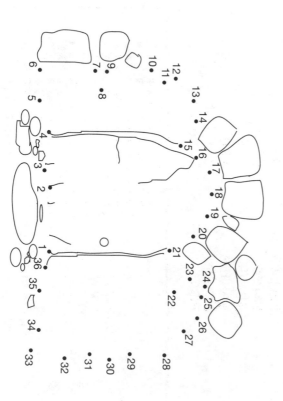

COLOR THIS PICTURE

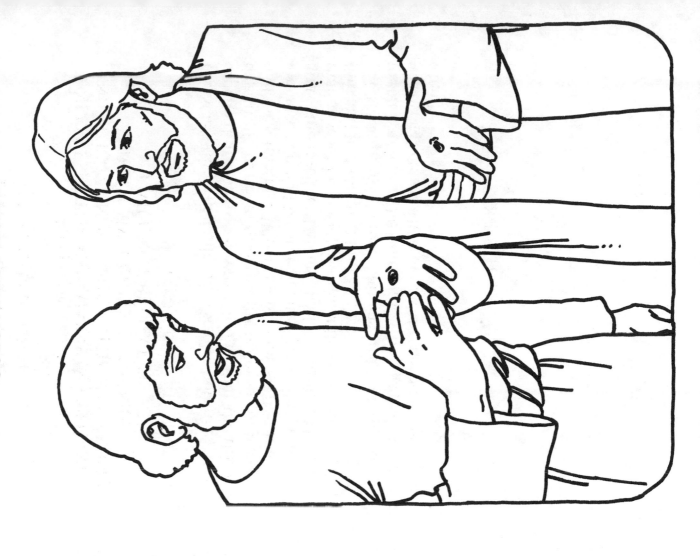

WORD SEARCH

```
K I K Q V S B R P Q S S W G G
W K V M E C K Y C S M E D I N
G B G E B B C R D P K E J V I
B K N T Q R E Z Q X W I Z E T
O K S O H A M L L G Z Z A L B
R X E R L O O X I O P O W X U
A B H X E Q M P H E B B Z R O
V H L Y S G X A O W V H A F D
K L Q E L L N O S R X E T E R
G Q C F S C I V T Z B D E N
Z K N A D S H A F L K I A W M
X O Q L N S E A N T S C U Q C
Q I T W D P W D N O H B E K Q
F S Z P L S X D C D I Q N O K
```

WORD LIST

BELIEVE
DOUBTING
HAND
REACH
SIDE

BLESSED
FINGERS
NAILS
SEEN
THOMAS

FIND THE RIGHT WORD

1. SAD
2. DOUBTED
3. JESUS
4. JESUS

ANSWERS

THOMAS DOUBTS
BASED ON JOHN 20:24-30

Scripture for Today

UNLESS I SEE THE NAIL MARKS IN HIS HANDS
AND PUT MY FINGER WHERE THE NAILS WERE,
AND PUT MY HAND INTO HIS SIDE,
I WILL NOT BELIEVE IT.

John 20:25b

LESSON—Jesus had told his disciples before he was crucified that he would return to life after the third day. In their grief and sorrow the followers of Jesus had forgotten this. When it was reported that Jesus was alive and had been seen after three days in the grave, the disciple, Thomas, had his doubts. He said that he would believe Jesus was alive only when he saw him and had touched him.

Jesus appeared before Thomas and told him to touch him so that he would know he was real. Thomas was overwhelmed when he saw the Lord and believed what he saw.

CONNECT THE DOTS

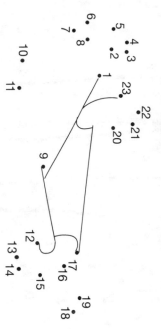

FIND THE RIGHT WORD

1. Thomas was _____ that Jesus was crucified.

  happy   sad   mad

2. When told Jesus was alive Thomas _____.

  shouted   hid   doubted

3. Thomas said he wanted to touch _____ and then he would believe.

  Jesus   Paul   David

4. _____ told Thomas to reach out and touch him.

  Stephen   Moses   Jesus

DRAW A PICTURE

COLOR THIS PICTURE

WORD SEARCH

```
M H N H A T H D M R
G O S T V E J B O H
G V S D X K G H T C
C N H E L S R A H T
J H I R S A W Y E I
G W I Y E B B D R P
G A G D R V M T N C
O T E C D C I W A F
O E Z G D E V R I R
G R I V A K N K J C
```

WORD LIST

BASKET   CRYING
HIDDEN   MOSES
MOTHER   PITCH
RIVER   TAR
WATER

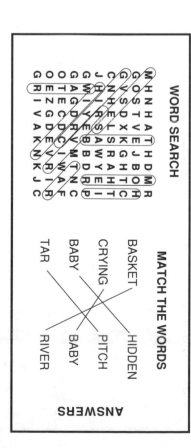

WORD SEARCH

MATCH THE WORDS

BASKET — HIDDEN
CRYING — PITCH
BABY — BABY
TAR — RIVER

ANSWERS

BABY IN A BASKET

BASED ON EXODUS 2:1-10

Scripture for Today

SHE PLACED THE CHILD IN IT AND
PUT IT AMONG THE REEDS
ALONG THE BANK OF THE NILE.

Exodus 2:3c

LESSON—The Pharaoh, who was like a king, decided that all the Hebrew boy children under the age of two should be put to death. Moses was a little baby, near and dear to the heart of his mother. His mother made a basket, sealed it with tar and pitch so that it would not leak, and placed baby Moses in the basket. Setting the basket in the water, she placed it where it would be found. The daughter of Pharaoh found the basket and took Moses into her home and raised him.

MATCH THE WORDS THAT GO TOGETHER

BASKET   HIDDEN

CRYING   PITCH

BABY   BABY

TAR   RIVER

DRAW A PICTURE OF THE PRINCESS
FINDING BABY MOSES

COLOR THIS PICTURE

DRAW A PICTURE FROM TODAY'S
SCRIPTURE LESSON

TRUE OR WORD SCRAMBLE
FALSE
1. TRUE   ENVY
2. TRUE   PATIENT
3. TRUE   KIND
             PROUD

ANSWERS

THE MEANING OF LOVE

BASED ON 1 CORINTHIANS 13:4-13

Scripture for Today

AND NOW THESE THREE REMAIN:
FAITH, HOPE AND LOVE. BUT
THE GREATEST OF THESE IS LOVE.

1 Corinthians 13:13

LESSON—The Apostle Paul told the early Christians that love was the most important part of the Christian life. He said that love was kind and considerate. Love is patient and does not anger easily or do evil to another person. Paul said that all of us need to learn how to love as Jesus loved us.

UNSCRAMBLE THE WORDS

NEVY

TENTIPA

DINK

DROUP

TRUE OR FALSE

1. Love is kind to others.

2. Love is not proud.

3. We should all love one another.

DRAW A PICTURE OF SOMETHING YOU LOVE

COLOR THIS PICTURE

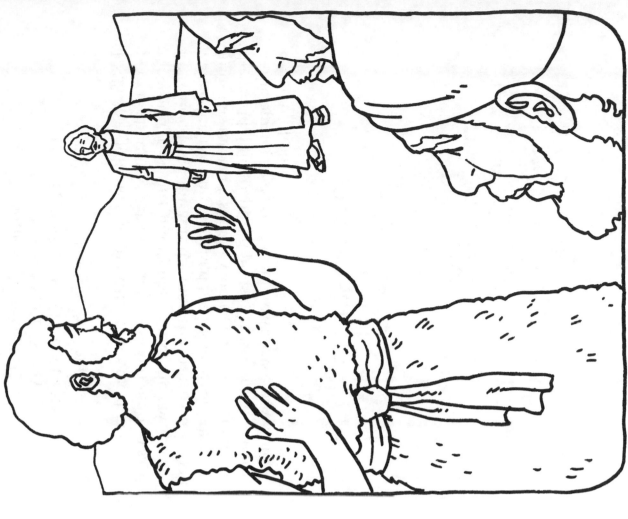

WORD SEARCH

```
K I K S W T N Q V B
R P I A Q I S H S W
G N T W K R L V O M
C E K S Y I C A S J
R D M E U P D I M G
B G O B C S R D D B
P K E V J V E O B K
Q R Z Q E X G J W I
Z E O K O A M L G Z
Z A L R X E L O X O
```

WORD LIST

DOVE   GOD
JESUS   JOHN
LAMB   SIN
SPIRIT   WATER

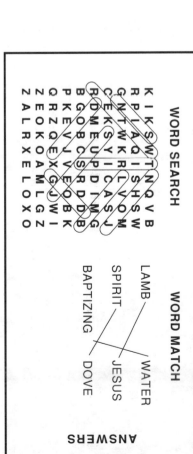

JOHN MEETS JESUS

<u>BASED ON JOHN 1:24-34</u>

Scripture for Today

I HAVE SEEN AND TESTIFY
THAT THIS IS THE SON OF GOD.

John 1:34

LESSON—John was down by the water teaching people about the person that God would send to save the world from sins and trouble. When he saw Jesus, he realized that this was the man the entire world had waited for, the one promised by God. He said that Jesus was the lamb sent by God to take away the sin of the world. John baptized Jesus that day and watched as the Spirit came down from heaven as a dove and rested on Jesus.

CONNECT THE DOTS

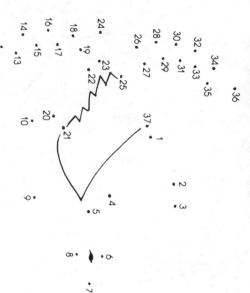

MATCH THE WORDS THAT GO TOGETHER

LAMB   WATER

SPIRIT   JESUS

BAPTIZING   DOVE

DRAW A PICTURE

COLOR THIS PICTURE

WORD SEARCH

```
C S M E D I G B D G B C
P R H D P K E Y J R V B
K R W E Q R Z Q E X O W
I J E I V Z E O K B O L
A M O A C E L G Z Z O A
L R X N C K N E L O X F
O P O W A H E I X A L H
X Q P H B H B D N E Z R
V H Y O X O W H E A F K
L Q L O G R X T G Q C F
```

WORD LIST

GO
LORD
OBEY
WICKED

FLEE
JONAH
NINEVEH
PREACH

WORD SEARCH

```
C S M E D I G B D G B C
P R H D P K E Y J R V B
K R W E Q R Z Q E X O W
I J E I V Z E O K B O L
A M O A C E L G Z Z O A
L R X N C K N E L O X F
O P O W A H E I X A L H
X Q P H B H B D N E Z R
V H Y O X O W H E A F K
L Q L O G R X T G Q C F
```

TRUE OR
FALSE

1. TRUE
2. TRUE
3. FALSE
4. TRUE
5. TRUE

ANSWERS

From *Children's Bulletins*. Copyright © 1992 Abingdon Press. Used by permission.

26

JONAH RUNS FROM GOD

BASED ON JONAH 1:1–2:10

Scripture for Today

IN MY DISTRESS I CALLED TO THE LORD,
AND HE ANSWERED ME.

Jonah 2:1*b*

LESSON—God instructed Jonah to go to the city of Nineveh and to tell the wicked people to change their ways. Jonah was afraid to go because he feared the people and so he ran away. Jonah boarded a ship and sailed in the other direction. A storm came up and the sailors were afraid God would destroy them. Jonah confessed that God was angry with him because he did not obey God. The sailors threw Jonah overboard and a big fish swallowed him. He was inside the belly of the fish for three days and then God told the fish to spit Jonah up onto land. Jonah finally did go to Nineveh to tell the people what God said.

TRUE OR FALSE

1. Jonah was a prophet of God.

2. Jonah was afraid to obey God.

3. The sailors threw Jonah in jail.

4. A large fish spit Jonah up and onto shore.

5. Jonah finally obeyed God.

DRAW A PICTURE OF TODAY'S STORY

COLOR THIS PICTURE

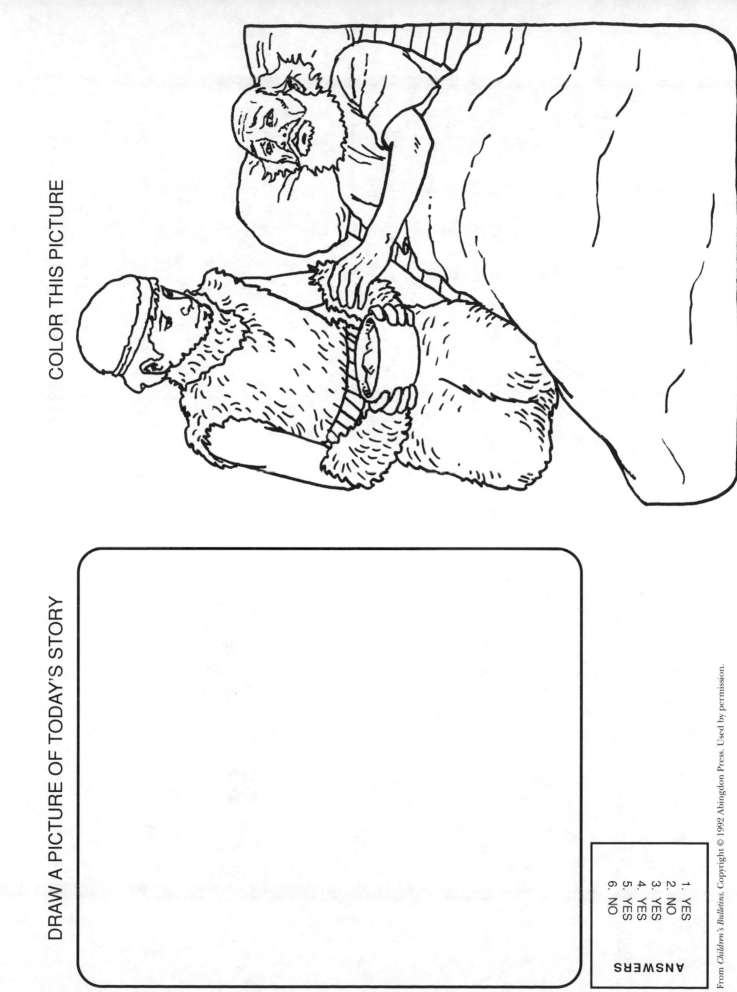

DRAW A PICTURE OF TODAY'S STORY

From *Children's Bulletins*. Copyright © 1992 Abingdon Press. Used by permission.

JACOB LIES TO HIS FATHER

BASED ON GENESIS 27:5-29

Scripture for Today

COME NEAR SO I CAN TOUCH YOU, MY SON,
TO KNOW WHETHER YOU REALLY ARE
MY SON ESAU OR NOT.

Genesis 27:21b

LESSON—Isaac was an old man. He was very wealthy and poor in health. He intended to leave his older son, Esau, all of his wealth. When Esau went out hunting game to make his father his favorite stew, Jacob and his mother, Rebekah, came up with a plan so that Jacob would have the inheritance.

Rebekah and Jacob made a stew for Isaac and dressed Jacob up to look like Esau. Jacob's skin was smooth and soft, but Esau was hairy and had a rough complexion. Rebekah covered Jacob's hands and neck with goatskin while he took some of his brother's clothes and dressed up like Esau.

At first the old man, who was almost blind, did not believe this to be his older son, Esau. But, after a time, he believed. As he ate the stew that had been prepared for him, Jacob asked for his father to bless him. Isaac did so and said that all that he had would belong to him. Rebekah and Jacob had lied to gain the family fortune and Isaac was fooled.

When Esau came home and learned what had happened he was very hurt and angry.

CONNECT THE DOTS

YES OR NO

1. Isaac was a very old man.

2. His younger son, Jacob, wanted what belonged to his brother Abner.

3. Rebekah helped Jacob fool Isaac.

4. Jacob put on a disguise to fool Isaac.

5. Jacob took some stew to his father and asked for the family blessing.

6. Isaac saw through the disguise and shot Jacob with his bow.

COLOR THIS
PICTURE

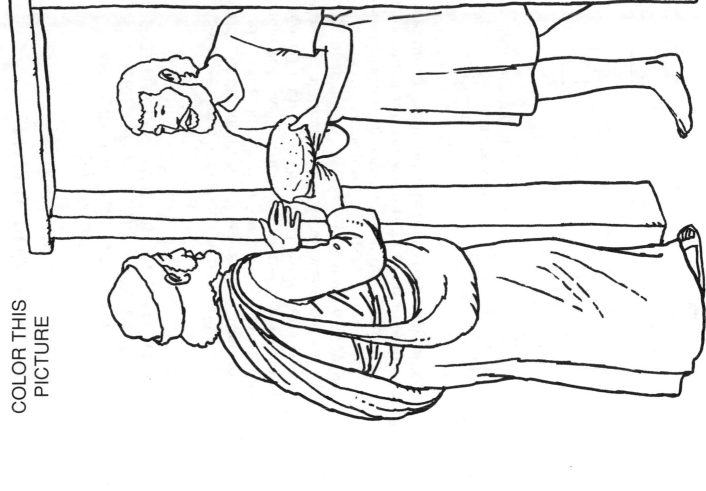

WORD SEARCH

```
M E D I G B G B
J C R B D P K E
J O V B R K H M
Q R U Z Q E I X
D W I R L D A K
E Z E P N O E D
E K O I A E M L
N G G Z S Z Y A
L H R X E L O X
T O P O W X A H
```

<u>WORD LIST</u>

BREAD   HELP
JOURNEY   MIDNIGHT
NEED   SEEK

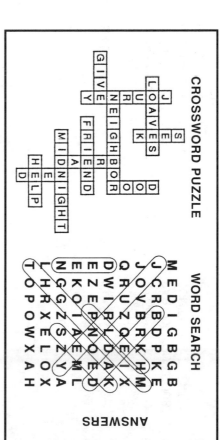

CROSSWORD PUZZLE

WORD SEARCH

ANSWERS

From *Children's Bulletins*. Copyright © 1992 Abingdon Press. Used by permission.

I NEED BREAD!

BASED ON LUKE 11:5-13

Scripture for Today

ASK AND IT WILL BE GIVEN TO YOU;
SEEK AND YOU WILL FIND; KNOCK
AND THE DOOR WILL BE OPENED TO YOU.

Luke 11:9b

LESSON—A man was called out of town during the middle of the night. Needing bread, he went to his neighbor and knocked on the door. The neighbor would not open his door to give the man the bread he needed for the trip. The man kept on knocking and asking until the neighbor finally went to the door and gave the man the bread he needed for his journey. In telling us this story, Jesus tells us that you won't always get what you want by asking, but if you stay determined and know it is right to do something then good things will happen because you stuck with it.

MAZE

Help the man find his way to the door with the bread.

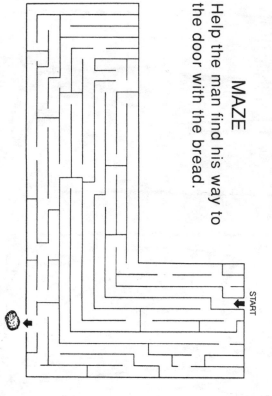

START

CROSSWORD PUZZLE

ACROSS CLUES

3. ———— OF BREAD
5. PERSON WHO LIVES NEXT DOOR
7. OFFER TO ANOTHER
8. SOMEONE SPECIAL
9. A LATE HOUR
11. A CRY FOR ————

DOWN CLUES

1. LOOK FOR
2. A LONG TRIP
4. PART OF YOUR HOUSE
6. SOMETHING TO EAT
10. I ———— ———— BREAD!

COLOR THIS PICTURE

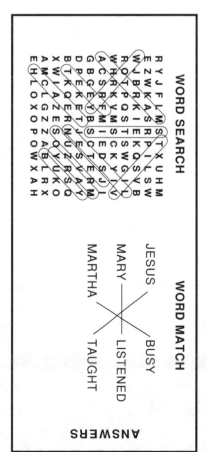

WORD SEARCH

```
R Y J F L M S T X U H M
E Z W K A S R P I L S W
W J B R K I E K Q S V B
R O T P Q S T S W G I L
W H R K V M S C K Y I V
A C S R F M I E D S J I
G B G E Y B S C T E R M
D P E K E T J E S V A Y
B T K Q E R N U Z R S Q
X W I A Z E S O Y U K O
A M C L G Z Z A B L R X
E H L O X O P O W X A H
```

WORD LIST

BUSY	FEET
JESUS	LISTEN
MARTHA	MARY
SISTERS	TEACH
VISIT	WORRY

From *Children's Bulletins*. Copyright © 1992 Abingdon Press. Used by permission.

MARY AND MARTHA
BASED ON LUKE 10:38-42

Scripture for Today

MARY HAS CHOSEN WHAT IS BETTER, AND IT WILL NOT BE TAKEN AWAY FROM HER.

Luke 10:42b

LESSON—Jesus had gone to Bethany to visit two friends, Mary and Martha. The two women were sisters of Lazarus and they were very glad to see Jesus. Martha got so caught up in making things right for Jesus' visit that she did not take time to stop and listen to the conversation Jesus was having. She was trying to make everything perfect for the Lord. Mary, on the other hand, stopped what she was doing and listened to the Lord.

When Martha saw that Mary was not helping but sitting at the Lord's feet listening to him, Martha complained about her sister not helping. Instead of asking Mary to go help Martha, the Lord told her that Mary was right to stop and listen and learn.

MATCH THE WORDS THAT GO TOGETHER

JESUS	BUSY
MARY	LISTENED
MARTHA	TAUGHT

DRAW A PICTURE OF TODAY'S STORY

COLOR THIS PICTURE

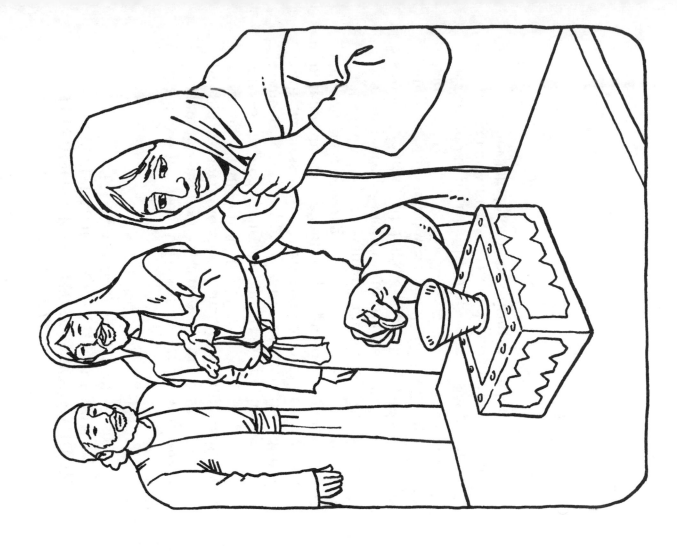

CONNECT THE DOTS

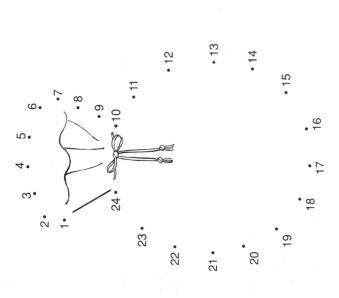

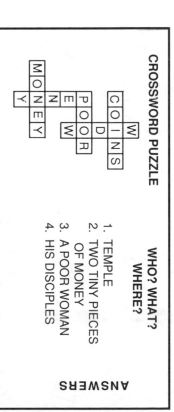

CROSSWORD PUZZLE

WHO? WHAT?
WHERE?

1. TEMPLE
2. TWO TINY PIECES
   OF MONEY
3. A POOR WOMAN
4. HIS DISCIPLES

ANSWERS

A WIDOW'S GIFT

BASED ON MARK 12:41-44

Scripture for Today

I TELL YOU THE TRUTH, THIS POOR WIDOW
HAS PUT MORE INTO THE TREASURY
THAN ALL THE OTHERS.

Mark 12:43b

LESSON—Jesus and his disciples went to worship in the temple. Just inside the doors were chests where people dropped the money that they brought as a way of saying "thank you" to God.

Jesus watched as the people left their offerings. Some were very happy. Their faces seemed to shine with gladness. Others were not happy. They gave only because they wanted other people to see them making their offering.

Finally a very poor woman came in. She dropped two tiny pieces of money into the chest. Her face shone. She was glad that she was able to give God an offering. Although it was a small gift, it was all she had.

Jesus said to his friends, "This woman has given more than anyone else. The rich have given and still have money left; but she has given all she has to live on."

WHO? WHAT? WHERE?

1. Where had the poor widow gone to worship? _____

2. What did she put in the offering? _____

3. Who was this story about? _____

4. Who was Jesus telling about this woman's good deeds? _____
_____

CROSSWORD PUZZLE

ACROSS CLUES

2. A PENNY AND A DIME
3. NOT RICH
4. USED TO BUY THINGS

DOWN CLUES

1. THIS WOMAN WAS A _____
3. ONE CENT

COLOR THIS PICTURE

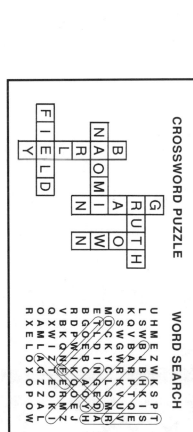

WORD SEARCH

```
U H M E Z W K S P T
L S W B J B H K I S
K Q V B A R P T Q E
S S W G W R K V U V
M D C K Y C L S M R
E T L D I N G E D A
B G O E B C A O Y H
R D P W I K O O E J
V B K Q N F E R M Z
Q X W I Z T E O K I
O A M L A G Z Z A L
R X E L O X O P O W
```

<u>WORD LIST</u>

ATE   BARLEY
FIELD   FOOD
HARVEST   NAOMI
RUTH   TOWN

From *Children's Bulletins*. Copyright © 1992 Abingdon Press. Used by permisson.

CROSSWORD PUZZLE

```
        G
    B   R U T H
  N A O M I   W
  A R   N   A O
  O L       N
F I E L D
  Y
```

WORD SEARCH

```
U H M E Z W K S P T
L S W B J B H K I S
K Q V B A R P T Q E
S S W G W R K V U V
M D C K Y C L S M R
E T L D I N G E D A
B G O E B C A O Y H
R D P W I K O O E J
V B K Q N F E R M Z
Q X W I Z T E O K I
O A M L A G Z Z A L
R X E L O X O P O W
```

ANSWERS

NAOMI AND RUTH

BASED ON RUTH 2:1-18

Scripture for Today

RUTH GLEANED IN THE FIELD UNTIL EVENING.

Ruth 2:17

LESSON—Ruth and her mother-in-law lived alone in the land of Moab. They were poor and had no family in the area. To get food for the two of them, Ruth would go to the fields and gather loose pieces of barley to make bread. When she had enough for a meal she would return home and share what she had with her mother-in-law. God blessed the two women as Ruth took care of the older woman's needs.

MAZE

Show Ruth how to find the field that has enough grain for a meal.

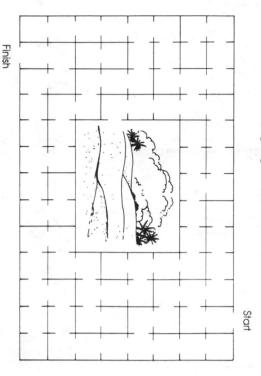

Start

Finish

CROSSWORD PUZZLE

ACROSS CLUES

2. NAOMI'S DAUGHTER-IN-LAW
5. THE OLDER LADY IN THE STORY
6. WHERE GRAIN WAS FOUND

DOWN CLUES

1. OATS AND BARLEY
3. A PLACE TO LIVE
4. A KIND OF GRAIN

DRAW A PICTURE

COLOR THIS PICTURE

DRAW A PICTURE OF TODAY'S STORY

**CHOOSE
THE WORDS**

1. FOLLOWED
2. CARED
3. DISCIPLES
4. TWO
5. THANKS
6. PLENTY

ANSWERS

A PICNIC WITH JESUS

BASED ON MATTHEW 14:13-21

Scripture for Today

THEY ALL ATE AND WERE SATISFIED.

Matthew 14:20a

LESSON—People seemed to follow Jesus almost anywhere he went. Thousands followed him to hear his teachings. As evening came the disciples realized there was no food to feed them. Finding a boy with two fish and five loaves of bread they took it to Jesus. Jesus gave thanks to God for the food and told the disciples to hand out food to all who were hungry. When they finished feeding the multitudes of people there was still plenty of food left over. The apostles gathered the extra food to show how God had provided for the people.

MAZE

Help the disciples find the people and give them food.

START →

→ END

COLOR THIS PICTURE

CHOOSE THE WORDS

1. The people _____ Jesus.

   ran from   followed   hid from

2. Jesus _____ about the people being hungry.

   cried   worried   cared

3. The disciples _____ wanted to send the people away.

   priest   governor

4. They learned there were _____ fish and five loaves of bread that one person had brought.

   six   five   two

5. Jesus gave _____ for the food and the disciples passed it out to the people.

   money   thanks   clothing

6. Everyone had _____ to eat.

   nothing   little   plenty

COLOR THIS PICTURE

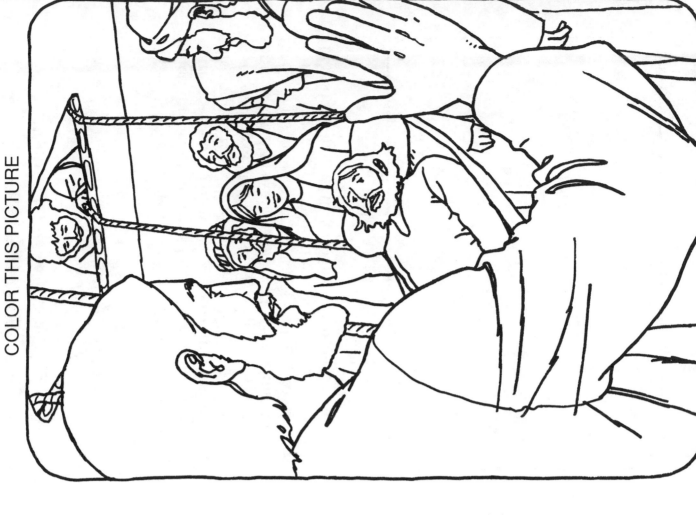

CROSSWORD PUZZLE

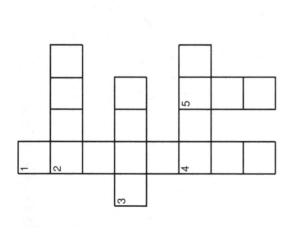

ACROSS CLUES

2. TOP PART OF A HOUSE
3. A WAY TO TRAVEL
4. WHERE YOU LIVE

DOWN CLUES

1. TO TELL ABOUT
5. SOMETHING TO LAY ON

CROSSWORD PUZZLE

P			
R	O	O	F
E			
W	A	L	K
	C		
	H	O	M	E
		E		A
				T

1. TRUE
2. TRUE
3. TRUE
4. FALSE

TRUE OR
FALSE

WHO? WHAT?
WHERE? HOW?

1. JESUS
2. TO A HOUSE
3. HIS FRIENDS LOWERED
   HIM THROUGH A HOLE
   IN THE ROOF
4. HE HEALED HIM AND
   FORGAVE HIS SINS

ANSWERS

JESUS HEALS

BASED ON MARK 2:1-12

Scripture for Today

SON, YOUR SINS ARE FORGIVEN.

Mark 2:5c

LESSON—Jesus traveled to the city of Capernaum. When the people learned he had come home they went to see him. The house was crowded with people who wanted to see Jesus. A man who was paralyzed wanted to be healed by Jesus. His friends removed some of the tiles in the roof and lowered him down through the hole in the roof. When Jesus saw this he went to the man and told him his sins were forgiven. He told the man to pick up his mat and go home.

DRAW A PICTURE

WHO? WHAT? WHERE? HOW?

1. Who went to Capernaum? _____

2. Where did he go? _____

3. How did the paralyzed man get to see Jesus? _____
_____

4. What did Jesus do for the man? _____
_____
_____

TRUE OR FALSE

1. People followed Jesus everywhere he went.

2. The house Jesus was staying in was too crowded for anyone else to get in.

3. Some men removed tile from the roof and lowered their friend down to see Jesus.

4. Jesus refused to forgive the man's sins.

COLOR THIS PICTURE

WORD SEARCH

T Z P G G L H C N A L
J I W Q O S Q E N O S
F E A U R Q O T N M E D
T X R D I Y I A U H N Z
Z P N U C S S F C O D Z
N Q A O S O U N E W H G
Y A A L H A A S O A N S
A T N C M R L R E I S E
S U S O B S C E K J E T
W S C C Y I A E M K E B

WORD LIST

BRANCHES   COATS
CROWD   FEAST
HOSANNA   JERUSALEM
JESUS   KING
LORD   PALMS
SHOUT

WORD SEARCH

T Z P G G L H C N A L
J I W Q O S Q E N O S
F E A U R Q O T N M E D
T X R D I Y I A U H N Z
Z P N U C S S F C O D Z
N Q A O S O U N E W H G
Y A A L H A A S O A N S
A T N C M R L R E I S E
S U S O B S C E K J E T
W S C C Y I A E M K E B

ANSWERS

From *Children's Bulletins*. Copyright © 1992 Abingdon Press. Used by permission.

35

JESUS GOES TO JERUSALEM

BASED ON JOHN 12:12-14

Scripture for Today

**BLESSED IS HE WHO COMES
IN THE NAME OF THE LORD!**

John 12:13c

LESSON—On the day that Jesus went to Jerusalem the people were very happy. They believed that he was the one sent from God to save them from their troubled lives. Jesus entered the village riding a young donkey. The people shouted words of praise and laid their coats and palm leaves on the ground before him to show him how happy they were he had come.

CONNECT THE DOTS

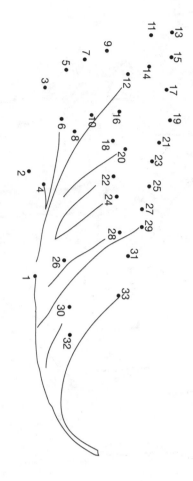

DRAW A PICTURE

COLOR THIS PICTURE

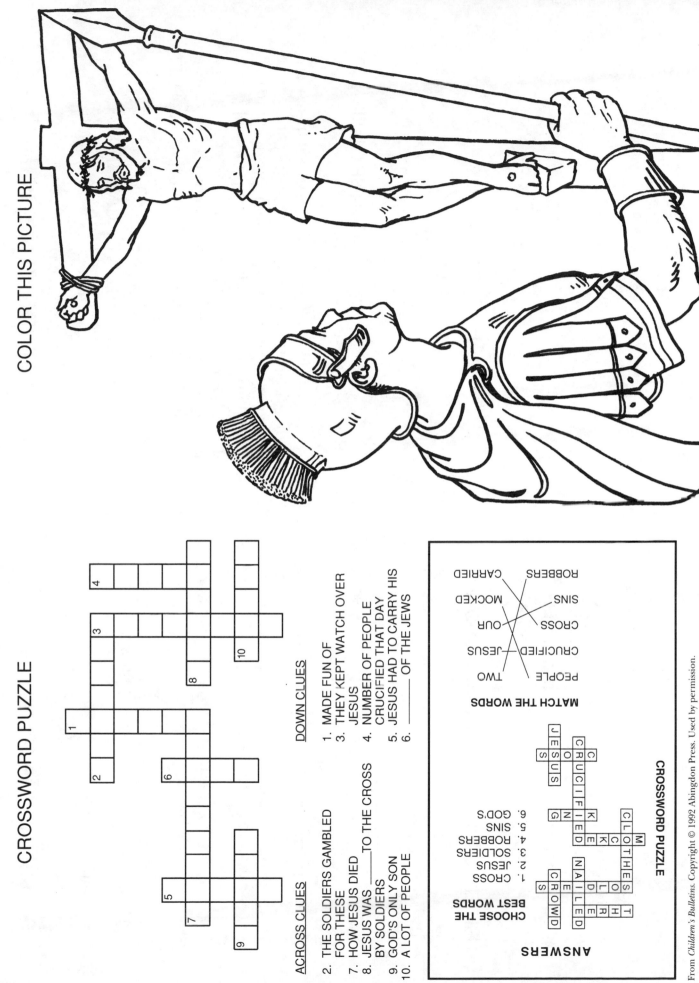

CROSSWORD PUZZLE

ACROSS CLUES

2. THE SOLDIERS GAMBLED FOR THESE
7. HOW JESUS DIED
8. JESUS WAS _____ TO THE CROSS BY SOLDIERS
9. GOD'S ONLY SON
10. A LOT OF PEOPLE

DOWN CLUES

1. MADE FUN OF
3. THEY KEPT WATCH OVER JESUS
4. NUMBER OF PEOPLE CRUCIFIED THAT DAY
5. JESUS HAD TO CARRY HIS
6. _____ OF THE JEWS

MATCH THE WORDS

PEOPLE — TWO

CRUCIFIED — JESUS

CROSS — OUR

MOCKED — SINS

ROBBERS — CARRIED

CHOOSE THE BEST WORDS

1. CROSS
2. JESUS
3. SOLDIERS
4. ROBBERS
5. SINS
6. GOD'S

CROSSWORD PUZZLE

```
        M
  C L O T H E S   T
  R     C     C   H
  U     R     L O C K E D
  C     O     O   R
  I     S     T   E
  F     S     H   D
  I           E N A I L E D
  E J E S U S     S
  D       O
    C R O W D
```

ANSWERS

From *Children's Bulletins*. Copyright © 1992 Abingdon Press. Used by permission.

36

JESUS IS CRUCIFIED

BASED ON MATTHEW 27:32-50

Scripture for Today

FOR HE SAID, I AM THE SON OF GOD.

Matthew 27:43

LESSON—What a sad day for the world. Jesus was beaten by his captors and sentenced to death on a cross for crimes that he did not commit. The soldiers nailed Jesus to the cross and there Jesus died for the sins of the world. One of the soldiers looked at Jesus as he hang helplessly on the cross and said, "Surely this was the Son of God."

CONNECT THE DOTS

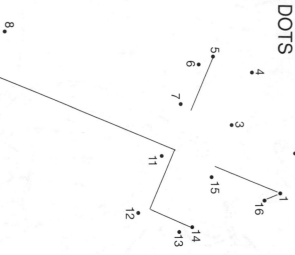

CHOOSE THE BEST WORDS

1. Jesus was made to carry his own _____.

   sword   food   cross

2. The crowd wanted _____ crucified.

   Paul   Jesus   John

3. The _____ cast lots for his clothing.

   soldiers   bankers   priest

4. Two _____ were crucified on each side of Jesus.

   merchants   robbers   fishermen

5. Jesus was crucified for the _____ of the world.

   money   sins   rest

6. Jesus is _____ son.

   God's   David's   Paul's

MATCH THE WORDS THAT GO TOGETHER

PEOPLE	TWO
CRUCIFIED	JESUS
CROSS	OUR
SINS	MOCKED
ROBBERS	CARRIED

COLOR THIS PICTURE

DRAW A PICTURE OF TODAY'S STORY

MATCH
THE WORDS

PEOPLE —— TWO
CRUCIFIED —— JESUS
CROSS —— OUR
SINS —— MOCKED
ROBBERS —— CARRIED

WORD
SCRAMBLE

1. CRUCIFIED
2. FOLLOWERS
3. WOMEN
4. THERE
5. RISEN

ANSWERS

JESUS LIVES AGAIN!

BASED ON MATTHEW 27:62–28:10

Scripture for Today

HE HAS RISEN FROM THE DEAD.

Matthew 28:7a

LESSON—Jesus had promised that when he was killed he would come back to life after three days. For those three days those who loved him mourned his death. They seemed so caught up in their sorrow that they forgot his promise to return to them. On the third day Mary Magdalene and Mary visited the tomb where Jesus had been buried. An angel told them Jesus was not there, that he had risen from the dead. The women ran to tell the others.

MAZE

Help the women find their way to the tomb.

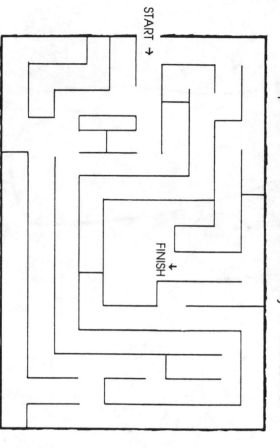

START →

FINISH ↓

WORD SCRAMBLE

1. Jesus was _____ fiedciruc .

2. His _____ llofweors were very sad.

3. The _____ mowen went to visit the tomb.

4. Jesus was not _____ reeth .

5. Jesus had _____ siren as he had promised.

MATCH THE WORDS THAT GO TOGETHER

PEOPLE   TWO

CRUCIFIED   JESUS

CROSS   OUR

SINS   MOCKED

ROBBERS   CARRIED

COLOR THIS PICTURE

DRAW A PICTURE

FILL IN BLANKS

1. Joseph
2. father
3. jealous
4. coat
5. killed

MATCH THE WORDS	
JACOB	ISRAEL
FATHER	JEALOUS
BROTHERS	KILLED
GOAT	COAT

ANSWERS

A BEAUTIFUL NEW COAT

BASED ON GENESIS 37:1-34

HIS BROTHERS WERE JEALOUS OF HIM.

Scripture for Today

Genesis 37:11a

LESSON—Joseph was greatly loved by his father. His father made him a coat of many colors and gave it to him as a gift. Joseph's brothers were very jealous of him. When they got a chance they captured him, stole his beautiful coat, smeared it with goat's blood and sold their brother into slavery. The men took Joseph's beautiful coat to his father and told him that his favored son had been killed. Jacob was filled with sorrow and mourned the death of his son, not knowing that he had been taken to Egypt where he would become a powerful man.

CONNECT THE DOTS

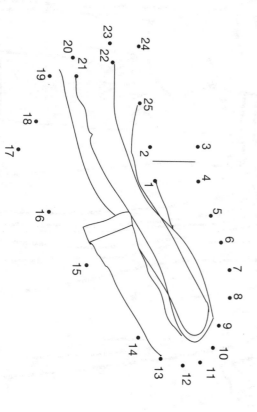

FILL IN THE BLANKS

1. _____ was his father's favorite son.

   Jacob   Joseph   David

2. Joseph's _____ made him a beautiful coat as a gift.

   mother   brother   father

3. The brothers became _____ of Joseph.

   jealous   friends   bitter

4. They took his _____ and smeared blood on it.

   pants   coat   horse

5. Jacob thought his son had been _____ .

   killed   sloppy   robbed

MATCH THE WORDS THAT GO TOGETHER

JACOB   ISRAEL

FATHER   JEALOUS

BROTHERS   KILLED

GOAT   COAT

COLOR THIS PICTURE

CROSSWORD PUZZLE

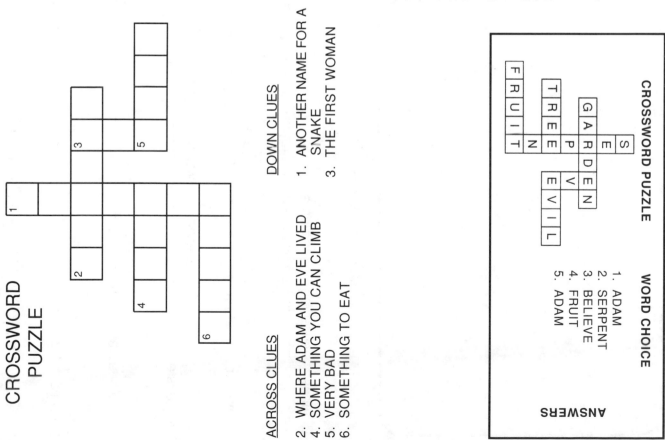

ACROSS CLUES

2. WHERE ADAM AND EVE LIVED
4. SOMETHING YOU CAN CLIMB
5. VERY BAD
6. SOMETHING TO EAT

DOWN CLUES

1. ANOTHER NAME FOR A SNAKE
3. THE FIRST WOMAN

CROSSWORD PUZZLE

WORD CHOICE

1. ADAM
2. SERPENT
3. BELIEVE
4. FRUIT
5. ADAM

ANSWERS

IN THE GARDEN

BASED ON GENESIS 3:1-6

Scripture for Today

YOU MUST NOT EAT FRUIT FROM THE TREE THAT IS IN THE MIDDLE OF THE GARDEN.

Genesis 3:3

LESSON—God gave Eve fair warning to stay away from the tree in the middle of the garden of Eden. He told her not to eat it's fruit or she would surely die. The serpent was crafty and sneaky. He appealed to Eve's sense of wanting something she should not have by telling her it would be good for her. Eve believed the serpent and did not believe God. She took the fruit from the tree and ate it and then she gave some to Adam to eat. Adam and Eve were not only the first couple, they were also the first humans to disobey God and to sin.

MAZE

Help Eve find her way through the garden.

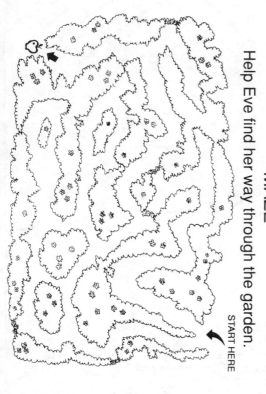

START HERE

CHOOSE THE RIGHT WORDS

1. Eve lived with _____ and _____ in the garden.

   the serpent   Adam   Cain

2. The _____ was smart and crafty.

   serpent   tree   donkey

3. Eve chose to _____ the serpent.

   follow   believe   eat

4. Eve took the _____ of the tree and ate it.

   bark   syrup   fruit

5. After eating the fruit she gave some to _____ .

   the serpent   her sons   Adam

DRAW A PICTURE

COLOR THIS PICTURE

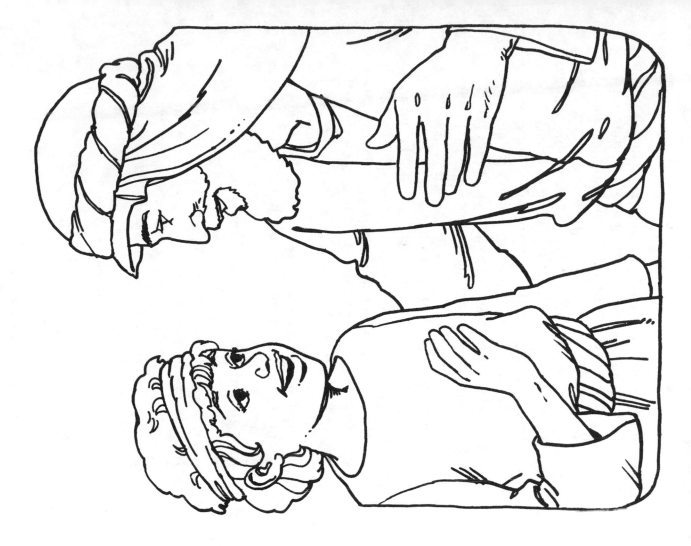

DRAW A PICTURE FROM TODAY'S
SCRIPTURE LESSON

From *Children's Bulletins.* Copyright © 1992 Abingdon Press. Used by permission.

THE BOY SAMUEL

BASED ON 1 SAMUEL 3

Scripture for Today

"HERE I AM; YOU CALLED ME."

1 Samuel 3:8

LESSON—Hannah was very sad because God had never sent her a baby. One day she prayed, "Dear Father, please send me a baby boy. I will love him and take good care of him. When he is older, he can help the priest in the temple."

God answered Hannah's prayer, and sent her a baby boy. Hannah held the baby close to her heart and thanked God for him. She named him Samuel. She did not forget her promise that Samuel could help the priest in the temple.

In those days, travel was very hard and helpers often stayed for a while in the temple with the priest. Samuel went to the temple to stay with a very kind priest, Eli. Eli taught Samuel about God and about God's love for little children. There were many things Samuel could do for Eli, because Eli was a very old man. Whenever Eli called, Samuel ran to him.

One night when Samuel had been asleep, he thought he heard Eli calling. Samuel jumped up and ran to Eli, but Eli said: "I did not call you, my son. Lie down again." After this had happened three times, Eli knew that it was God speaking to Samuel. "Go and lie down," he said to Samuel. "If you hear the voice again, answer; for God wants to tell you something."

Samuel lay down again, and he heard the voice calling. He answered, "Speak for your servant is listening." So God talked to Samuel and told him what he wanted him to do.

FILL IN THE BLANKS

1. Hannah _____ wanted a baby very much.

   Hannah   Ruth   Sue

2. God _____ Samuel.

   spoke to   forgot   left

3. Eli told _____ to listen for God's voice.

   Goliath   David   Samuel

4. Samuel did as _____ had said.

   God   Joshua   Eli

MAZE

Help Samuel find his way to Eli.

START

FINISH

COLOR THIS PICTURE

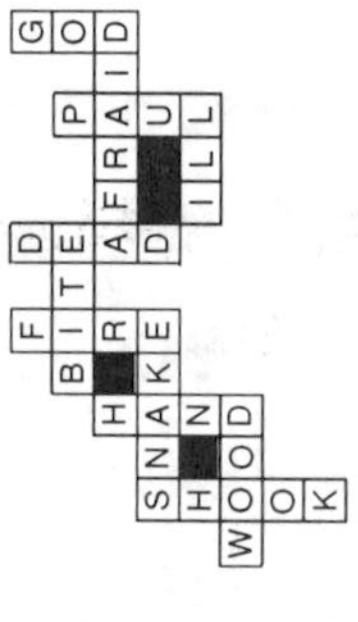

WORD SEARCH

```
W I Z E O K O A D M L G
Z H G Z A L R X E A L O
X O A N P O D S W X E A
H X Q N I P H O N B B D
Z S R V D G H Y G A B X
O W H H D A N F K I K F
L L Q O O L O A T R I E
X T U G O Q C E H R F C
V T Z A W K B N E Z K N
A D L K P L L I W M X O
```

WORD LIST

BITE	DEAD	GOD
FIRE	HAND	HANGING
ILL	PAUL	SNAKE
SHOOK	WOOD	

From *Children's Bulletins*, Copyright © 1992 Abingdon Press. Used by permission.

ANSWERS

WORD SEARCH

CROSSWORD PUZZLE

WORD SCRAMBLE

MALTA
SNAKE
WOOD
PAUL
FIRE

PAUL AND THE SNAKE

BASED ON ACTS 28:1-6

Scripture for Today

BUT PAUL SHOOK THE SNAKE OFF INTO THE
FIRE AND SUFFERED NO ILL EFFECTS.

Acts 28:5

LESSON—Paul was with a group of men on an island named Malta. Paul gathered a pile of brushwood, and as he placed it on the fire, a snake crawled out and onto the hand of Paul. The men were very afraid because they thought God was punishing Paul. But Paul shook the snake off his hand and was not bitten by the snake.

CONNECT THE DOTS

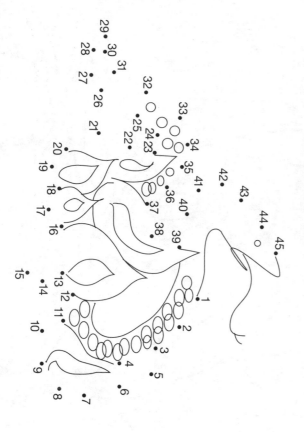

CROSSWORD PUZZLE

<u>ACROSS CLUES</u>

4. TAKE A —————
7. SCARED
8. WHAT PAUL SHOOK
   OFF HIS HAND
9. SICK
10. USED TO MAKE A FIRE

<u>DOWN CLUES</u>

1. A BRIGHT LIGHT
2. NOT ALIVE
3. THE ONE WE WORSHIP
5. THE MAN THIS STORY IS ABOUT
6. IT HAS FINGERS
8. PAUL —————— THE SNAKE OFF
   HIS HAND

UNSCRAMBLE THE WORDS

LAMTA

SKNAE

DOWO

APUL

RIFE

COLOR
THIS
PICTURE

DRAW A PICTURE OF TODAY'S STORY

MATCH THE WORDS

GIANT ———— BEHEADED

GOLIATH ⨯ SLINGSHOT

DAVID ———— BULLY

ANSWERS

DAVID MEETS GOLIATH

BASED ON 1 SAMUEL 17:1-58

Scripture for Today

GO, AND THE LORD BE WITH YOU.

1 Samuel 17:37*b*

LESSON—Goliath was nothing more than a big Philistine bully. He stood over nine feet tall and because he was so tall everyone was afraid of him, everyone except David. David went to King Saul and asked to be allowed to go out and meet Goliath on the battlefield. The king agreed, and as David stepped forward everyone laughed at him. Goliath was ready to cut David's head off with his sword. Instead, David gathered a few smooth stones for his slingshot and slung one at Goliath. He killed the giant Goliath and became a hero among his people.

MATCH THE WORDS THAT GO TOGETHER

GIANT   BEHEADED

GOLIATH   SLINGSHOT

DAVID   BULLY

CONNECT THE DOTS

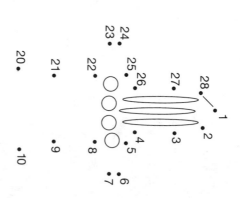

COLOR THIS PICTURE

WORD SEARCH

```
Y X O L S Y S X V V
F H P T B U Y P F Q
P I E F S R S G P H
N N S E N S E W S S
O U J H T S I A T P
M M X O E D I A K C
I F R C V R O N A D
S I L N O B M T K F
R S V W W I C E N I
C H U O D H H T N G
```

WORD LIST

BOATS   BREAK
CATCH   FISH
FISHERMEN   JESUS
NETS   SIMON
SINK

WORD SEARCH

```
Y X O L S Y S X V V
F H P T B U Y P F Q
P I E F S R S G P H
N N S E N S E W S S
O U J H T S I A T P
M M X O E D I A K C
I F R C V R O N A D
S I L N O B M T K F
R S V W W I C E N I
C H U O D H H T N G
```

ANSWERS

A NET FULL OF FISH

BASED ON LUKE 5:48

Scripture for Today

PUT OUT INTO DEEP WATER, AND LET DOWN THE NETS FOR A CATCH.

Luke 5:4

LESSON—Simon had been fishing all night long. He had no fish in his nets and was discouraged. Jesus told Simon to go back out onto the lake and let the nets back down and he would catch fish. Simon believed Jesus and obeyed his command. When he pulled up the nets they began to break because there were so many fish.

CONNECT THE DOTS

DRAW A PICTURE OF SIMON CATCHING FISH

COLOR
THIS PICTURE

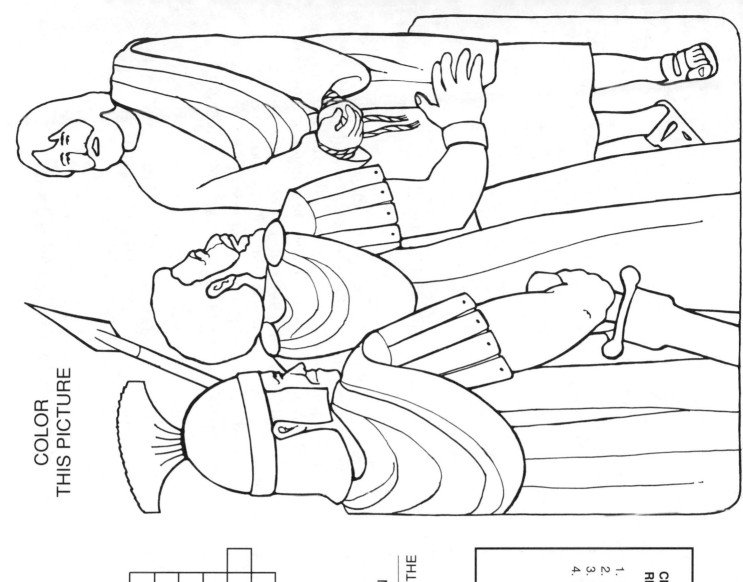

CROSSWORD PUZZLE

ACROSS CLUES

4. NUMBER OF DISCIPLES
5. 60 MINUTES
7. A PLACE TO WORSHIP
10. ___ CHRIST
11. IT HAS FINGERS
12. TO SMACK ON THE LIPS
13. NOT LIGHT
14. HE BETRAYED JESUS

DOWN CLUES

1. SHARP WEAPONS
2. ROUND WEAPONS
   LIKE A BAT
3. TURN ONE'S BACK ON
6. NOT TWO BUT ___
8. OLDER MEMBERS OF THE
   PRIESTHOOD
9. INQUIRE

CHOOSE THE
RIGHT WORD

1. MANY
2. JUDAS
3. SWORD
4. SERVANT'S

CROSSWORD PUZZLE

	S	C	B					
H	O	U	R					
	N	A	R		T	E	M	P	L	E
J	E	S	U	S		W	E	L	V	E
			K	I	S	S		A	H	A	N	D
			S			Y		E	D	A	R	K
			J	U	D	A	S					

ANSWERS

From *Children's Bulletins*. Copyright © 1992 Abingdon Press. Used by permission.

JESUS IS ARRESTED

BASED ON LUKE 22:47-53

JUDAS, ARE YOU BETRAYING THE SON OF MAN WITH A KISS?

Scripture for Today

Luke 22:48b

LESSON—As Jesus had said, the night came when he fell captive to his enemies. Judas, one of the twelve disciples, took money and showed those who wanted to kill Jesus where to find Him. When they found Jesus the soldiers arrested him. One of the disciples drew a sword to protect Jesus and cut off the ear of the high priest's servant. But Jesus touched the man's ear and healed him. The soldiers led Jesus away.

CONNECT THE DOTS

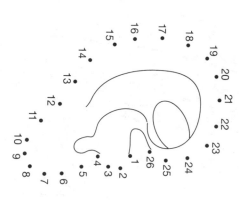

CHOOSE THE RIGHT WORD

1. When Jesus was arrested there were ———— people with him.

     many   few   no

2. ————————— betrayed him by giving him a kiss.

     Thomas   Paul   Judas

3. One of Jesus' disciples drew a ———— to protect him.

     picture   sword   elephant

4. The ———————— ear was cut off by a disciple.

     servant's   governor's   judge's

DRAW A PICTURE FROM TODAY'S SCRIPTURE LESSON

COLOR THIS PICTURE

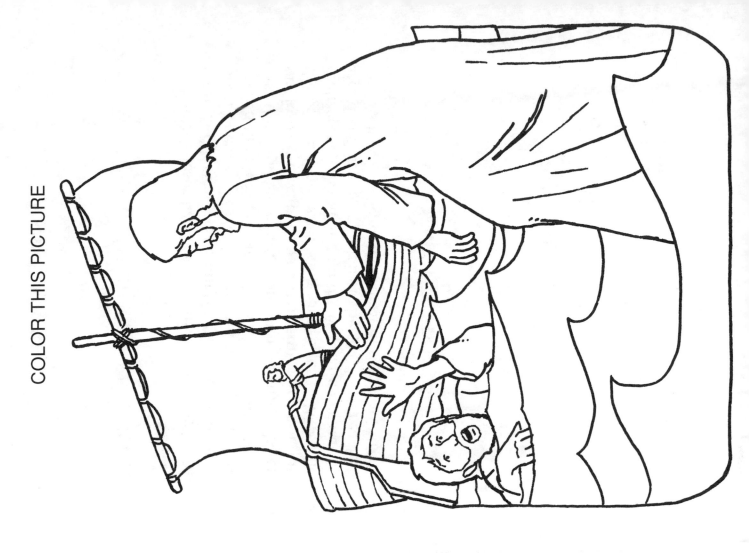

WORD SEARCH

```
E Z W K S P L T S W J B
K I K Q V B A R D W P Q
S L S W W O Y G A R W K
V M A A B A C L K Y O D
C S V K R M K E D I L
G E B P E E C G B S S C
S R D P D O K E C T J W
V B K Q U R Z I O Q A X
W I Z R E O P R K T O A
M L A G Z L M Z E A L R
X G E L E O X R O P O W
E X A S H X Q P H B B Z
```

WORD LIST

BOAT
DISCIPLES
LORD
STORM
WATER

COURAGE
LAKE
PRAY
WALKED
WAVES

WORD SEARCH

```
E Z W K S P L T S W J B
K I K Q V B A R D W P Q
S L S W W O Y G A R W K
V M A A B A C L K Y O D
C S V K R M K E D I L
G E B P E E C G B S S C
S R D P D O K E C T J W
V B K Q U R Z I O Q A X
W I Z R E O P R K T O A
M L A G Z L M Z E A L R
X G E L E O X R O P O W
E X A S H X Q P H B B Z
```

ANSWERS

A STORMY SEA

BASED ON MATTHEW 14:22-33

Scripture for Today

TAKE COURAGE! IT IS I. DON'T BE AFRAID.

Matthew 14:27*b*

LESSON—Jesus had been alone and praying. It was night and he wanted to join the disciples in their boat. The disciples looked up and saw Jesus walking toward them on the water. They were afraid. Jesus told them to have courage and not be afraid. Peter saw Jesus and wanted to be with him, so he got out of the boat and began walking toward Jesus. When he realized he was walking on the water, he became afraid and began to sink into the sea. Jesus reached out his hand and caught Peter and they got into the boat.

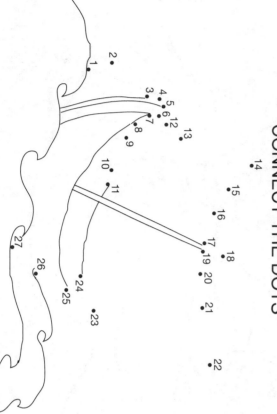

CONNECT THE DOTS

MAZE

Help Peter find his way to Jesus.

Start

DRAW A PICTURE

COLOR THIS PICTURE

WORD SEARCH

```
A  B  E  S  N  Y  P  O  S  L  C  I  V  X  M
L  F  V  O  W  C  Z  P  P  S  W  J  G  F  O
B  J  H  P  C  H  E  G  N  W  K  O  C  O  D
J  M  R  Y  G  J  A  F  L  D  O  X  U  H  G
M  E  Z  W  K  R  S  R  E  D  P  L  S  W  N
J  B  K  I  S  K  O  W  V  Q  V  B  R  P  I
Q  E  S  S  W  D  O  W  G  E  W  K  V  M  K
C  K  N  Y  C  S  E  P  S  M  S  E  D  I  G
B  D  E  E  S  G  U  E  B  C  R  T  D  P  K
E  J  V  B  M  L  K  Q  W  R  Z  Q  X  W  I
Z  E  O  K  L  Y  O  A  M  L  G  Z  Z  A  L
R  X  E  L  O  X  O  P  O  W  X  A  H  X  Q
P  H  B  B  Z  R  V  H  Y  X  O  W  H  A  F
```

WORD LIST

ENEMY   GOOD
GROW   HARVEST
KINGDOM   PULL
SEED   SOWED
WEEDS

WORD SEARCH

```
A  B  E  S  N  Y  P  O  S  L  C  I  V  X  M
L  F  V  O  W  C  Z  P  P  S  W  J  G  F  O
B  J  H  P  C  H  E  G  N  W  K  O  C  O  D
J  M  R  Y  G  J  A  F  L  D  O  X  U  H  G
M  E  Z  W  K  R  S  R  E  D  P  L  S  W  N
J  B  K  I  S  K  O  W  V  Q  V  B  R  P  I
Q  E  S  S  W  D  O  W  G  E  W  K  V  M  K
C  K  N  Y  C  S  E  P  S  M  S  E  D  I  G
B  D  E  E  S  G  U  E  B  C  R  T  D  P  K
E  J  V  B  M  L  K  Q  W  R  Z  Q  X  W  I
Z  E  O  K  L  Y  O  A  M  L  G  Z  Z  A  L
R  X  E  L  O  X  O  P  O  W  X  A  H  X  Q
P  H  B  B  Z  R  V  H  Y  X  O  W  H  A  F
```

ANSWERS

PARABLE OF THE WEEDS

BASED ON MATTHEW 13:24-30

Scripture for Today

LET BOTH GROW TOGETHER UNTIL THE HARVEST.

Matthew 13:30

LESSON—Jesus told a story about how you can tell what is good and what is bad from each other. He said that if you plant wheat in a field you allow both the good wheat and the ugly weeds to grow together. He said that for a while they look the same, but when the time is right the farmer knows the grain from the weed and the weed will be pulled up and thrown away. So it is with those who love Christ and those who don't, they grow together but when the time comes God knows those who are his.

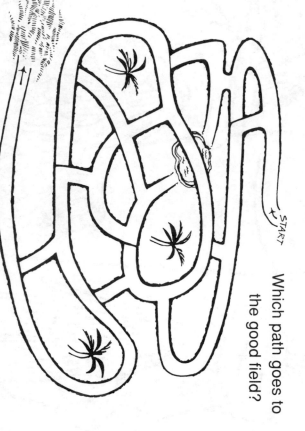

START

Which path goes to the good field?

DRAW A PICTURE FROM TODAY'S LESSON

COLOR THIS PICTURE

WORD SEARCH

```
C O J M R Y M S J F L X
N U H M E Z O W U K S P
D O L S W J D B D S K I
K E S Q V B G R P O E Q
S A S S W G N W K V G J
M V N S C K I Y C S B M
E D I G E I K G B I G N
B C R S E L D P R K E N
E J V B I L B T K W R Q
R Z Q X W T H I S O Z E
O K O A M L G Z B Z A L
R X E L O X O P O W X A
```

<u>WORD LIST</u>

ANGEL   BIRTH
BLESSED BORN
GOD   JESUS
KINGDOM NEWS
SON   VISIT

WORD SEARCH

```
C O J M R Y M S J F L X
N U H M E Z O W U K S P
D O L S W J D B D S K I
K E S Q V B G R P O E Q
S A S S W G N W K V G J
M V N S C K I Y C S B M
E D I G E I K G B I G N
B C R S E L D P R K E N
E J V B I L B T K W R Q
R Z Q X W T H I S O Z E
O K O A M L G Z B Z A L
R X E L O X O P O W X A
```

TRUE OR
FALSE

1. TRUE
2. TRUE
3. TRUE
4. FALSE

ANSWERS

AN ANGEL VISITS MARY

BASED ON LUKE 1:28-33

Scripture for Today

GREETINGS, YOU WHO ARE HIGHLY FAVORED! THE LORD IS WITH YOU.

Luke 1:28

LESSON—God sent an angel to give Mary the good news. God had selected Mary to be the mother of God's only child. Mary was a young girl and did not understand how this was possible. The angel told her that God was with her and she would have a son and name him Jesus.

CONNECT THE DOTS

TRUE OR FALSE

1. An angel came to visit Mary one night.
2. The angel told her God was with her.
3. He told her that she would be the mother of God's only son.
4. The angel said to name the baby Stephen.

DRAW A PICTURE

COLOR THIS PICTURE

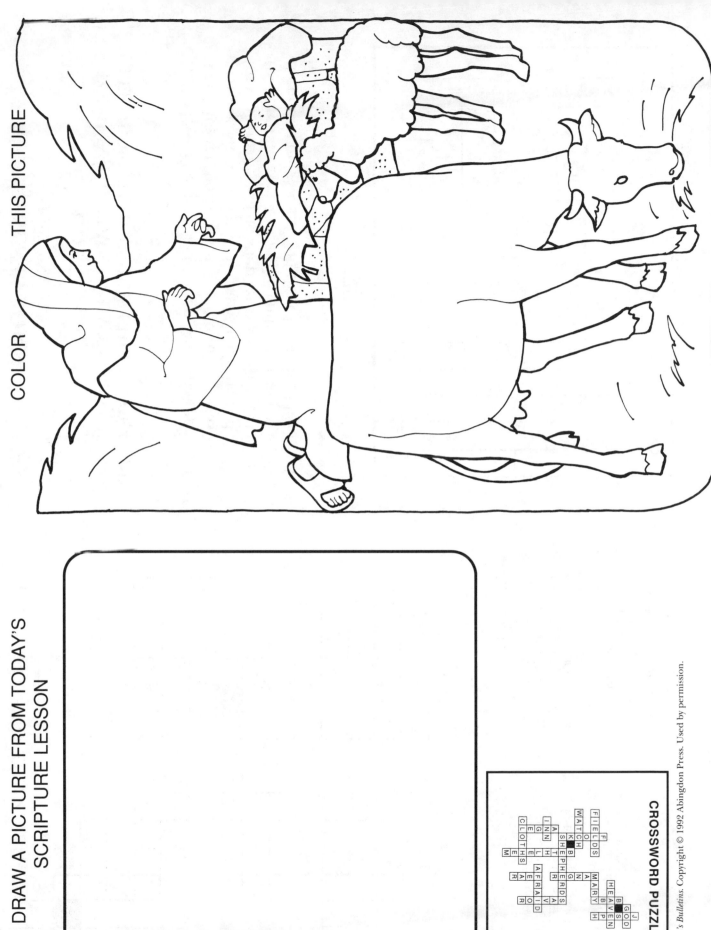

DRAW A PICTURE FROM TODAY'S
SCRIPTURE LESSON

CROSSWORD PUZZLE

ANSWERS

JESUS IS BORN

BASED ON LUKE 2:4-20

TODAY IN THE TOWN OF DAVID A SAVIOR HAS BEEN BORN TO YOU; HE IS CHRIST THE LORD.

Scripture for Today

Luke 2:11

LESSON—The time came when Mary had her baby. The baby was born in a stable and his bed was a manger. Mary wrapped the baby in cloths and laid him in a manger. The shepherds saw an angel who told them to go and find the child. The angel told them that they would find the Christ child lying in a manger.

MAZE

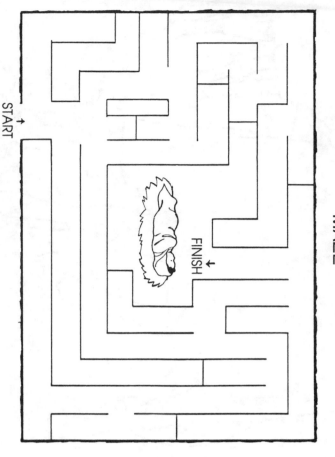

START →

FINISH →

CROSSWORD PUZZLE

ACROSS CLUES

2. GLORY BE TO ——
4. WHERE THE ANGELS WENT
6. WHERE THE SHEPHERDS KEPT THEIR SHEEP
7. MOTHER OF JESUS
8. TO LOOK AFTER
10. THEY TOOK CARE OF THE SHEEP
13. A KIND OF HOTEL
14. FEARFUL
16. JESUS WAS WRAPPED IN THESE

DOWN CLUES

1. HE MARRIED MARY
3. JESUS CAME TO US AS ONE
5. A BUNCH OF SHEEP
7. WHERE MARY LAY BABY JESUS
9. WHERE JESUS WAS BORN
11. WHAT JESUS IS TO US
12. A HEAVENLY BEING
15. TO BE AFRAID

COLOR THIS PICTURE

DRAW A PICTURE

From *Children's Bulletins*. Copyright © 1992 Abingdon Press. Used by permission.

FEED MY SHEEP

BASED ON JOHN 21:15-19

Scripture for Today
FEED MY SHEEP!

John 21:17c

LESSON—After Jesus was resurrected he appeared to the disciples. He came to give them instructions and to tell them they needed to tell others about Jesus. Jesus asked Peter if he loved him. Peter said that he did. Jesus said to Peter, "Feed my sheep." What that meant was to tell everyone about Jesus and share the good news of the gospel. When we love Jesus we should tell everyone about Jesus.

CONNECT THE DOTS

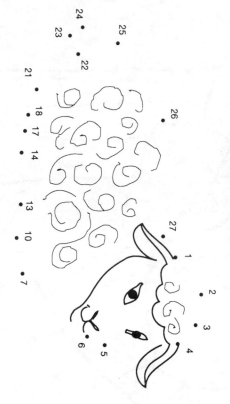

UNSCRAMBLE THE WORDS

PEESH

DEFE

WOLLOF

VOLE

DRAW A PICTURE FROM TODAY'S SCRIPTURE LESSON

COLOR THIS PICTURE

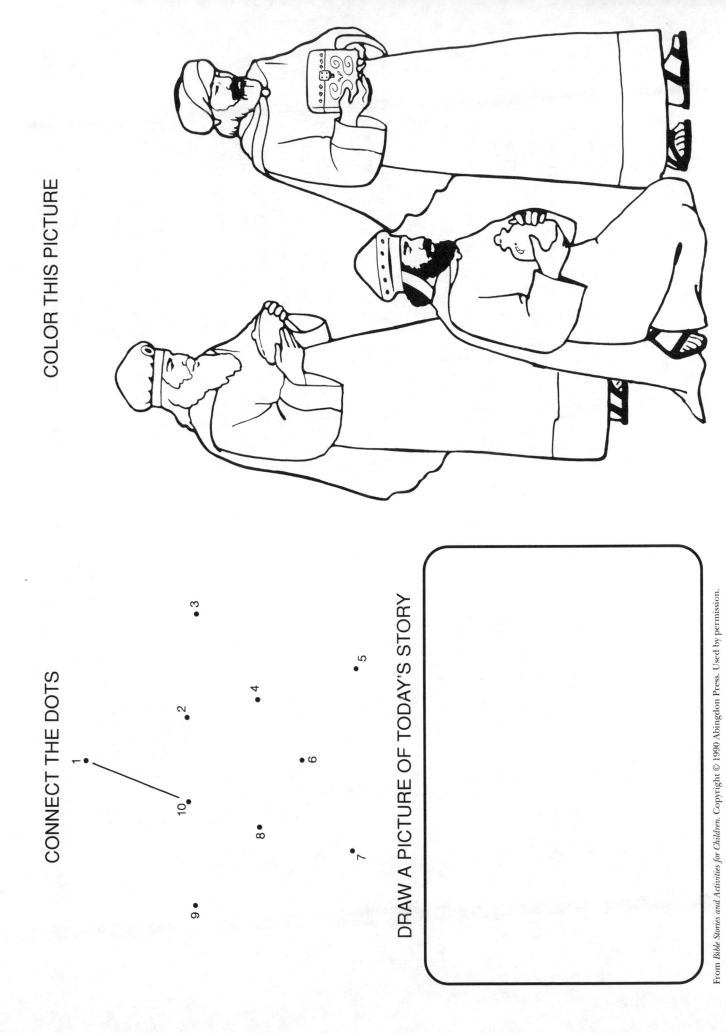

CONNECT THE DOTS

DRAW A PICTURE OF TODAY'S STORY

THE WISE MEN

BASED ON MATTHEW 2:1-12

Scripture for Today

WE SAW HIS STAR IN THE EAST AND HAVE COME TO WORSHIP HIM.

Matthew 2:2

LESSON—When Jesus was born some men far away from Bethlehem were watching the heavens. These wise men often studied the stars. Tonight they were surprised to see a strange, bright, new star. They decided that the star was giving them a message—a most wonderful message that a new king had been born.

They quickly prepared for a long journey. They traveled on camels' backs, and along with their food and clothes they brought special gifts for the baby king.

It wasn't an easy journey, and even when they reached Jerusalem no one knew about the king. "Where is the new king?" the wise men asked. But no one could tell them.

When night came the star once again showed the way, and the wise men quickly followed it until they reached the place where the baby Jesus and his earthly parents were staying. They had found him at last.

MAZE
Help the wise men follow the star to Bethlehem.

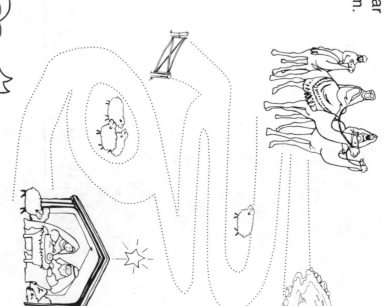

WHAT WOULD YOU GIVE THE BABY JESUS?

Draw a picture of your gift inside the box.

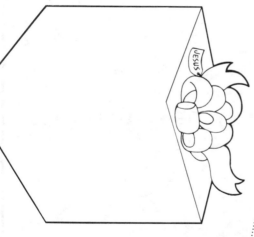

JESUS

COLOR THIS PICTURE

DRAW A PICTURE OF TODAY'S STORY

HELPING TO BUILD THE WALL

BASED ON NEHEMIAH 1:1-3; 6:1-16

Scripture for Today

THIS WORK HAD BEEN DONE
WITH THE HELP OF OUR GOD.

Nehemiah 6:16*b*

LESSON—Nehemiah lived in the king's palace and helped him. One day the king noticed that Nehemiah was very sad. "Are you ill?" he asked. Nehemiah explained to him that he was unhappy because some friends had come from his home in Jerusalem, and told him that their wall had been torn down, the gates of the city had been burned, and the people were in danger.

The king said in a kind voice, "Perhaps you should go home and see if you can help to rebuild the walls."

Nehemiah started at once. He was happy now. When he reached Jerusalem, he called all the people together. They were glad to see him. "We are in great trouble," he said. "Come, let us build up the walls so that we will be safe from thieves and wild animals. God will help us make our home safe and beautiful again."

It was a long, long wall and would take years to rebuild if only a few men worked, but everyone was willing to help. There were people on the outside of the wall who said, "You will never be able to finish this big job." But Nehemiah answered, "God is helping us. We are all working together, and we will finish."

The wall grew and grew and in less than two months, every gate was finished and every stone of the great wall was in place.

Nehemiah and his friends marched around the city, singing praises to God. They were joyful because each had helped and their city was once more a safe and beautiful place.

FILL IN THE BLANKS

1. Nehemiah lived in the king's _____.
   palace   basement   storeroom

2. He heard that the wall around _____ had been destroyed.
   Egypt   Damascus   Jerusalem

3. The wall was very _____.
   short   white   long

4. Nehemiah and his friends _____ around the city, _____.
   ran   crawled   marched
   singing   crying   laughing

MAZE
Help Nehemiah find his way home.

START HERE

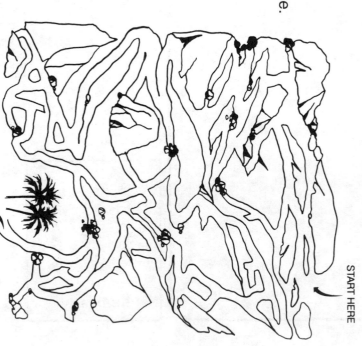

HOME

COLOR THIS PICTURE

WORD SEARCH

```
D N I L B J K Q P O
I H S E J E S U S N
K D A M A S C U S M
G C E F S A U L L U
L I G H T K A R T V
M A A N A N I A S K
```

WORD LIST

DAMASCUS	BLIND	
SAUL	LIGHT	
JESUS	ANANIAS	

FILL IN
THE BLANKS

1. DAMASCUS
2. JESUS
3. SIGHT
4. PAUL

WORD SEARCH

```
D N I L B J K Q P O
I H S E J E S U S N
K D A M A S C U S M
G C E F S A U L L U
L I G H T K A R T V
M A A N A N I A S K
```

ANSWERS

From *Children's Bulletins*. Copyright © 1992 Abingdon Press. Used by permission.

SAUL'S EXPERIENCE ON THE ROAD TO DAMASCUS

BASED ON ACTS 9:1-20

Scripture for Today

BE FILLED WITH THE HOLY SPIRIT.

Acts 9:17b

LESSON—Saul hated and feared the disciples of Jesus. One day he started out for Damascus to arrest the disciples there.

On the way, a light from heaven flashed around him and he fell to his knees in the road. Then he heard a voice, "Saul, Saul, why do you persecute me?"

"Who are you, Lord?" asked Saul.

The voice from within the light replied, "I am Jesus, whom you are persecuting. Go into the city and wait to hear what you must do."

Saul got up, but even though his eyes were open, he could see nothing. His friends took his hands and led him into Damascus. For three days he lay in a darkened room, neither eating nor drinking.

The Lord called Ananias, one of his disciples who lived in Damascus: "Go find a man named Saul. He is praying and he has seen a vision that you will come to him."

Ananias was afraid because he knew that Saul had come to arrest the followers of Jesus. Still, he went to Saul and laid his hands on him. "Brother," he said, "The Lord has sent me to you. Receive your sight and be filled with the Holy Spirit."

At once Saul could see. He spent several days with the disciples and began to proclaim that Jesus was the Son of God. He became known as the apostle Paul.

FILL IN THE BLANKS

1. Saul was on his way to _____ .

   Egypt   Damascus   Bethlehem

2. "I am _____ ," the voice said.

   Peter   Sam   Jesus

3. Saul lost his _____ .

   sight   hearing   touch

4. Later, Saul became known as _____ .

   Paul   Ananias   Eric

DRAW A PICTURE

COLOR THIS PICTURE

WORD SEARCH

```
C K Y C S M D E D I G B
G B C R D P E K D E J V
E G B K Q R S Z Q A X W
I C R Z E O S K D O L D
A P I E M L E G Z O R G
Z H E O A A L L R A G E
X E E O J T B L W O R T
X O P A P E O E K U E W
X A H X V L R E P A Q P
H B B Z R E E V C H Y X
O W H A F M N H K L Q L
O R X T G Q C F C V T Z
```

WORD LIST

BLESSED   GLAD
GOD   GREAT
HEAVEN   MEEK
PEOPLE   PURE
REJOICE   REWARD
TEACH

ANSWERS

MATCH
THE WORDS

HUNGER —— THIRST
COMFORTED ✕ HEART
PURE   MOURN

WORD SEARCH

JESUS TEACHES THE PEOPLE

BASED ON MATTHEW 5:1-12

Scripture for Today

REJOICE AND BE GLAD, BECAUSE
GREAT IS YOUR REWARD IN HEAVEN.

Matthew 5:12

LESSON—One day a great crowd of people followed Jesus to a mountainside. They wanted to hear what he had to say, because what he said made them understand more about God. Jesus told them that because they believed they were blessed in many ways. He also told them not to be discouraged when people gave them a hard time about their faith in God, because believing in God was the right thing to do and that someday they would be rewarded for believing.

MATCH THE WORDS THAT GO TOGETHER

HUNGER	THIRST
HEART	COMFORTED
MOURN	PURE

DRAW A PICTURE OF A WAY IN WHICH GOD
HAS MADE YOU FEEL GOOD ABOUT YOURSELF

COLOR THIS PICTURE

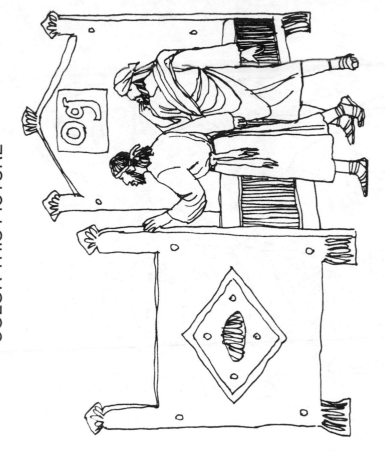

OG was a king
Who was tall and fat.
He was a giant—
Just think about that!

How big was Og's bed?

Deuteronomy 3:11

From *Aaron to Zerubbabel*. Copyright © 1987 Abingdon Press. Used by permission.

COLOR THIS PICTURE

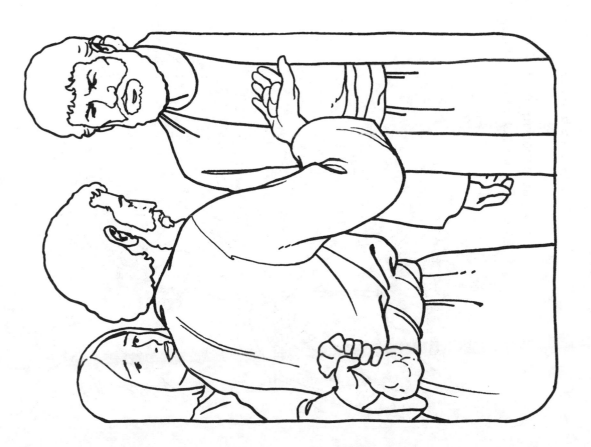

Is this a cheerful giver?

From *Children's Bulletins*. Copyright © 1992 Abingdon Press. Used by permission.

COLOR THIS PICTURE

What do you think is happening here?

COLOR THIS PICTURE

JEMIMAH's name means "little dove."
I bet she was full of peace and love.

Who was Jemimah's father?

Job 42:12-14